OFFSHORE

OFFSHORE

Tax Havens and the Rule of Global Crime

Alain Deneault

Translated from the French
by George Holoch

THE NEW PRESS

NEW YORK
LONDON

The New Press gratefully acknowledges the Florence Gould Foundation for supporting publication of this book.

Published in the United States by The New Press, New York, 2011
First published in France by La Fabrique éditions, Paris, 2010
Distributed by Perseus Distribution

LIBRARY OF CONGRESS CATALOGING-IN-PUBLICATION DATA

Deneault, Alain, 1970-
  [Offshore. English]
  Offshore : tax havens and the rule of global crime / Alain Deneault ; translated from the French by George Holoch.
    p. cm.
  Includes bibliographical references.
  ISBN 978-1-59558-648-3 (hc. : alk. paper) 1. Tax havens. 2. Informal sector (Economics) 3. Tax evasion. 4. International finance. 5. Sovereignty. I. Holoch, George. II. Title.
  HJ2336.D4613 2011
  336.24'316--dc23
                            2011020031

The New Press was established in 1990 as a not-for-profit alternative to the large, commercial publishing houses currently dominating the book publishing industry. The New Press operates in the public interest rather than for private gain, and is committed to publishing, in innovative ways, works of educational, cultural, and community value that are often deemed insufficiently profitable.

www.thenewpress.com

Composition by Influx House
This book was set in Baskerville and Franklin Gothic

Printed in the United States of America

10 9 8 7 6 5 4 3 2 1

CONTENTS

FOREWORD

Denying the law still means recognizing it.
And a pervert challenges it only so he can
give himself other laws.

— Mikel Dufrenne

Who leads? Who decides? This is the political question of the day.

For decades, predatory economic wars have consumed the global South and corrupted heads of state; ships flying flags of convenience have sent arms to the South and returned with the fruits of plunder; mercenaries have been mobilized by persons unknown; the drug traffic has in a few generations built fortunes as large as the GDP of nations; billions of dollars have vanished annually in a Bermuda triangle of dirty money; the originators of these investments have subsequently come forward under the leadership of "investors" in designer suits claiming to grasp everything; the public services of states of the North have been despoiled of funds matching the staggering profits heads of empires grant themselves; financial scoundrels have swallowed up the savings of entire populations and confronted no obstacles. Over all this time, it is clear that public institutions have lost control of the way the world works. Powerful actors have appeared offshore, outside the bounds of formal politics and law.

The reign of this "offshore sovereignty" implies that the primary decision makers in public affairs are no longer acting in the public arena. Instead, they have set up custom-made political jurisdictions—tax havens—that enable them to exercise decisive influence on the historical course of events without having to comply with any democratic principle. Subordinates in states governed by the rule of law join in the circus of election campaigns and the theater of legislative assemblies, and then all of that is assembled under the heading of "governance" to satisfy the people who witness these shadow plays. Even if the people don't believe these lies, it doesn't matter, because that is all they have a right to.

The effect of tax havens on the world can be measured here and now. Nothing is more erroneous, more restrictive, and more inappropriate than to limit the phenomenon to offshore, the mere negative idea of an "elsewhere" of finance, where capital flees and evades its holders, as though this exodus opened out onto parallel economies that observers insist on presenting as marginal and abnormal. These metaphors do not grasp the reality of tax havens, which are positive and sovereign political bases located offshore, where half the world's money supply is concentrated. The funds amassed there should not be thought of as the nest eggs rapacious financiers and industrial swindlers have stashed away, as pirates used to bury their treasure on islands. Nor should we think of misers, of which Honoré de Balzac writes in *Eugénie Grandet* that "they make heaps of their money to be able to gaze on it in secret." On the contrary, this money "works" without hindrance once it is placed in an offshore account, with no unions or professional regulations, no environmental measures, no bank supervision, no stock market framework, no real control over all kinds of trafficking, no knowledge on the part of the directors of private companies, and of course no taxation.

Along with these new spheres of power, suspect fortunes and dubious combinations grow up whose effects are felt directly in so-called democratic states. For example, companies that sell us retail gasoline are also involved in the arms trade; the banks in whose branches we deposit our savings also handle influence peddling for the benefit of frightful dictatorships. All financial and industrial actors of any size thereby have the opportunity to pay to advertise themselves with the benign face of Dr. Jekyll in the North while indulging offshore in the brew of Mr. Hyde. These "parallel economies" are nothing other than *our* economies.

In light of this organization of world finance, it is clear that the strict question of tax is the least compromising. To consider the offshore problem exclusively in terms of tax evasion is to overlook the way these transfers of money make it possible precisely to finance organizations, companies, and individuals together with the structures by means of which it has become ever easier for them to dominate states governed by the rule of law and to conduct their private politics outside the law. Tax evasion no longer means just saving money; it amounts to undermining the financing of public institutions, and hence the very notion of the public welfare, in order to establish offshore hidden centers of decision making on questions of historical importance.

A timid and fearful press, often itself in the pay of offshore interests, reports nothing of this. Concentrating its charges on the narrow problem of taxation in effect bars the press from considering the offshore phenomenon in all its magnitude. The same is true of the Organization for Economic Cooperation and Development (OECD), which, in the summer of 2009, together with the nations assembled as the G20, focused on and criticized tax evasion. According to the OECD, offshore states were required to provide access to secret accounts under very precise conditions. The United States tax authorities went after the tax-evasion tactics of UBS. That was all it took for the mainstream press to declare an end to the existence of tax havens without having really discussed them previously. States governed by the rule of law, after serving as providers of social insurance systems for major world banks and other sorcerer's apprentices of finance, were thereby attempting to recover the funds necessary for the minimal financing of their institutional structures—and to look good for public opinion.

But at its heart, the problem is too compromising for governing leaders to apply themselves to describing it, and it is therefore up to critical thinkers to bring these processes to light and reveal their modes of domination. The heuristic methods for accomplishing this are ill defined. Indeed, the offshore problem and the analysis of tax havens cannot be reduced to accounting, tax, or legal considerations. And it is hard to see how to approach it in general terms. To think through the offshore problem, we need a semantic reversal of the common notions of political thought: rule of law, political sovereignty, justice, law, crime, social classes, and economic rationality. In fact, the very meaning of these notions is affected by the worldwide offshore phenomenon. The rule of law as ordinarily understood is made unrecognizable when financial actors transform it from a resolutely domestic characteristic into an extra asset conferred on them by offshore sovereignty for dealing with world affairs. "Crime" and "ille-gality" are terms of little import when everything they previously covered is authorized and even encouraged in offshore jurisdictions whose full sovereignty is recognized and which sometimes sit with legitimate states on World Bank bodies or are recognized as full members of the European Union.

History now requires that we reverse our relationship with these words and therefore reconsider the concepts in connection with the way tax havens have affected them semantically. It is not possible to define tax havens without redefining, in light of their nature, the concepts used to arrive at that definition.

OFFSHORE

1

DEATH OF A FISCAL PRINCIPLE
PRIVATE WEALTH DEPENDS ON PUBLIC ORGANIZATION

Evade taxes, of course; avoid expenditure, it goes without saying; force the middle class to finance public infrastructures that benefit the financial elite, a good idea! But above all impoverish any institution other than those associated with high finance and large industry. Prevent any political body from being fully sovereign. Keep it under control, at the service of the interests of the oligarchy. The strategy of tax evasion makes the flight of capital offshore not only financially attractive but also politically relevant.

By the nineteenth century, as the modern state was establishing a tax system intended to finance major public works from which the elite profited and to constitute its armies to protect large private fortunes, the state was paradoxically subjected to pressure from the upper bourgeoisie. They caricatured the tax authority as a shameless body and transformed the issue of national tax collection into a false moral question. For what is known as the rule of law is not entirely the offspring of capitalist development. It is capable

of autonomous actions such as those inspired in the twentieth century by John Maynard Keynes and Thorstein Veblen.
It therefore seemed necessary to tie the rule of law to the
powerful interests of the new age. The United Kingdom established the model: speculators, investors, and landowners
led the dance of commercial life while the state and its common law merely supported, supervised, and if necessary ar-
bitrated their activities.[1] The business classes and the great
merchants therefore found it appropriate to keep this arbiter
of capital under close surveillance, by the holders of capital
themselves, and to deprive it of means of acting whenever it
took on airs as a major public decision maker. No real sovereignty was to be granted to a form of representation at the
expense of immediate interests.

Ruling, for this commercial and financial elite, meant
first of all having their own private information, maintaining secrecy over financial information and morally legitimat-
ing the culture of secrecy. Rhetoric was one of the weapons
of choice to impose this state of affairs. According to Georg
Simmel in "The Sociology of Secrecy and of Secret Societies,"
social functioning requires both disclosure and secrecy; the
rhetoric in question could not survive without elements of
both. The political issue was to determine the dividing line
between what was part of the public domain and what would
be confined to the secrecy of private life. The masters of high
finance took this distinction very seriously when it came to
matters of taxation, at the price of perverting the terms of
the debate. This was especially the case because the tendency
in the nineteenth century was toward increasing disclosure:
unprecedentedly, the state published its accounts and de-
manded that joint-stock companies do the same, so that informed investors could act accordingly. The era when power

cloaked itself in mystery to govern was over. The spread of the use of money in material transactions explains these measures requiring disclosure. These technical constraints give consistency to the principle that information has to be shared to allow for interactions of a social nature: "All relationships of people to each other rest, as a matter of course, upon the precondition that they know something about each other." Hence, through the demarcations presided over by the state we can grasp the outlines of the public and private spheres, and what appears is the dual tendency of liberal democracy, "that which pertains to the public becomes more public, that which belongs to the individual becomes more private."[2]

To throw a modest veil over issues that are basically political, the elite framed the debate in terms of moral considerations. The state, it was said, violates the privacy of corporations (considered "persons" under the law) and of citizens, as corporations were already being defined, by inquiring into the nature of their revenues and, moreover, deducting its share. In the scathing political campaigns the bourgeoisie orchestrated against it, the tax department, that intruder, was presented as inquisitorial, obscene, and voyeuristic. Arguing about the boundary between what belonged to the public domain and what could or should remain secret became an indispensable strategic enterprise. Enormous emphasis was laid on the principle articulated by Simmel that "concord, harmony, mutuality, which count as the socializing forces proper, must be interrupted by distance, competition, repulsion, in order to produce the actual configuration of society."[3] Because modesty and reserve turn out to be conditions of social life and communication, the bourgeois offensive against the tax system exhibited its moral claims by relying on the principle that secrecy is necessary for the functioning of society: administrative privacy was as valuable as privacy concerning intimate affairs. This meant setting financial issues in the private domain and assigning to the state the role of keeper of that secret. The liberal principle that publicly available information is sufficient to enable economic actors to pursue their interests rationally remains purely formal, playing a role only in editorials in the business press or university economics exams.

Hence, take advantage of the fact that our social mores acknowledge the irreducible necessity of secrecy and modesty in social interactions, place private financial affairs under the rubric of "ethics of discretion," and then identify as vulgarity any inclination of the tax authorities to inquire into personal assets—these are formulas that have worked down to the present, particularly among supporters of tax havens. According to this rhetoric, taxation, which enables the state to provide a minimum (and sometimes even less) representation of the public interest, is still presented as the "swindling" and "hypocrisy" in force in "bureaucratic heaven." The "fiscal hell" that states governed by the rule of law are said to have become, in the spirited description prevalent in such circles, undermines the family unit as the essential component of liberal democracy: "The state, wishing to take over the rights of the individual, has taken on an inquisitorial role in the modern world in pursuit of restrictive taxation complemented by a ruinous exchange control." Historical explanation permits all kinds of abusive comparisons, notably the identification of the tax inspector with the Gestapo, because Nazi Germany was the first state in history to require "German citizens to make a declaration of their overseas assets."[4]

These turns of phrase belong to the Swiss tax consultant Édouard Chambost, but they can also be found in the vast majority of books promoting tax evasion and international offshore centers. Grégoire Duhamel, for example, describes the European Union, manifestly dedicated to economic liberalism, as "Soviet" because it promotes the "crusades" of the state "inquisition" that foretell the "fatwas" of a "strangler" "Holy Tax," as demonstrated by the French wealth tax (Impôt sur la fortune, ISF), renamed for the purpose the "Imposition Socialo-fasciste." "To arms, taxmen; and forward, Marx!"[5]

In France in the 1980s André Harris, in *C'est la lutte fiscale* (The Tax Struggle), stigmatized France's "Catholic-Marxist cultural roots" to explain the "infernal process" to which the tax authorities subjected every honest citizen in the country. This convenient rhetoric supplies motives that justify taking refuge in tax havens: "It would be easy for me to have an account in Switzerland. . . . Lower the corporate tax rate to 30 percent and you will see fraud disappear," he promises, neglecting to mention that even if the rate he proposes were established, there would be a risk of further tax evasion because tax havens, immune from public expenses, anticipate collecting purely nominal taxes.[6]

In Canada, the author of *Take Your Money and Run* proposes in *My Blue Haven* the notion of "profligate" states and "avaricious" tax policies, directly identifying his fight against the tax system with fights against all the "injustices of this world."[7] For their part, Paul and Philippe DioGuardi have produced the gloomy *The Taxman Is Watching*, which opens with an anecdote of a tax collector pursuing a presumed fraud, although the "poor man" is on his deathbed, and goes on to explain why we have every reason to "be afraid" of the Canadian tax system.

This dark humor, filled with dubious historical comparisons and misconstrued philosophical citations, has become commonplace and has established terms of discourse that are ever more shameless. For example, Diane Francis, a distinguished spokesperson for the Canadian financial elite, regrets that tax evasion has brought the Canadian government to impose on its resident citizens a tax system of "socialist" inspiration. This is an implicit invitation to reverse the proposition: if Canada itself became a tax haven, it would not be necessary to flee its state tyranny.

The underlying logic is exposed in the economics textbooks used in business schools, even those that are financed by the state. *Multinational Business Finance*, published in the United States, devotes an entire chapter to tax havens so as to teach students how to "minimize the firm's international tax burden." This information is presented as being necessary. No political consideration is at issue; at most the text notes the existence of moral questions on the fringe of the imperatives of competition between commercial firms.[8]

This perversion of reasoning makes it possible not only to justify offshore centers but also to legitimate the suppression of any public representation, however weak, in the control or even understanding of financial affairs.

Along these lines, from the late nineteenth century to the present, world financial markets have insisted that they themselves should supervise, insofar as possible, the control of financial flows and the reputation of those who manage them. This explains the constant recurrence of "voluntary measures" and the durability of the principle of "self-discipline" that major industrial decision makers are encouraged to impose on themselves. Legitimate states subsequently suggest to financial players corresponding "incentives," as a supplement to real public control of world financial activities.

The principles of offshore laissez-faire stand as ramparts when the fight against tax havens goes beyond mere superficial gestures. Grégoire Duhamel thinks it appropriate that the OECD and the judicial bodies of the global North[*] record the "non-cooperating" tax havens in lists without political consequences. The lists established in 2000 by the OECD as well as by the Financial Stability Board (FSB) and the Financial Action Task Force (FATF), with the backing of the G7, did not erode in the least the international existence of bank secrecy and the massive operations of offshore finance. The 2009 attack, conducted in the aftermath of the economic crisis but in the planning for several years, was less laughable. This led to the exaggerated charge made whenever a state considers restrictive measures against capital: "While the first phase of the battle conducted by the OECD seems justified—record and moralize—the second, prohibit and punish, arises from pure ideology. This Rousseau-derived philosophy will no doubt come into conflict with the pragmatism of bankers and financiers who think about their clients and preserve the interests of the private sector."[9]

But according to Georg Simmel, identifying money as strictly personal property means misunderstanding its social significance. Rather, money functions as the element that depersonalizes relationships. For example, when ordinary financial activities are involved, it is customary for relevant in-

---

[*]Translator's Note: Throughout the book, the terms "North" and "South" designate areas formerly called the First World and the Third World.

formation to be published or controlled by a public body. This is especially the case because, due to the growth of credit, the capital circulating in the market seldom belongs personally to those who are manipulating it. Joint-stock companies or the beneficiaries of bonds and other debt instruments not only are playing with other people's money but also have the opportunity to grow rich thanks to the help of others. Under these circumstances, "that enlightenment which aims at elimination of the element of deception from social life is always of a democratic character."

Hence, taxation, the thorn in the side of the rich made possible by public control of information, reminds the privileged individual afflicted with unfathomable narcissism that personal wealth depends on collective organization: without a structured social context, there would be no possibility of harvesting profits all by oneself. "The right of . . . spiritual private property . . . can no more be affirmed in the absolute sense than that of material property. We know that in higher societies the latter, with reference to the three essential sides, creation, security, and productiveness, never rests merely upon the personal agency of the individual. It depends also upon the conditions and powers of the social environment."[10] Private ownership by a subject is explained by an established order of things; it is through various social organizations and institutions that the possibility arises for an individual to cultivate what will constitute his own set of secrets.

What ensues is a subject of political and historical debate. Where should the boundary between private and public be located? "No general norm can foresee" the delicacy and complexity of this philosophical question. Nor, with regard to taxation, does any universal unit of measurement make it possible to determine "the legal limits of an invasion" of privacy. This indeterminacy enables the die-hard advocates of discretion to say they are wronged as soon as one asks about their assets and to develop in response a multitude of offshore "financial products." Then they present the inviolable existence of bank secrecy as an attribute of civilization related to man's spiritual development and a defense against the inquisitorial barbarism of law-governed states. In this perspective, the "general law" is expressed as a restriction of property rights "by taxation."[11]

While invalidating the pertinence of taxation as a reminder of the public conditions of private wealth, the financial elite puts forward a contrary principle suited to its interests: the state survives institutionally only by tapping into private capital and the assets of individuals. So if private activity depends on public organization, the financing of public welfare depends in turn, structurally, on the products of private activity. Therefore the state is indebted, directly or indirectly, to the business class for the funds that enable it to exist. By depriving the state of its due, the business class reminds it of that fact.

2

RECOLLECTION OF SUPREME POWER

The masters of the first world economies in the Renaissance set up their headquarters in the great cities of Europe, thereby guaranteeing that they would escape completely from any taxation. In succession, they chose Antwerp, Venice, Genoa, and Amsterdam. At each stage, capital gave itself the tools and institutions necessary for its autonomous development.

The fifteenth century, the period when Venice was dominant, saw the introduction of checks, double-entry bookkeeping, and an accounting system that made possible the practically instantaneous movement of European capital. Organizational forms such as holding companies were also created, allowing third parties to bring together various investment funds, and intermediaries were eliminated from some transactions. Manufacturing industry followed suit. Instead of wealthy merchants, "the bankers were conveniently nearby, pen and notebook in hand. . . . Bookkeeping (*scritta*) was the miraculous method of settling transactions between merchants on the spot, by transferring payments, without the use of cash and without having to wait for the infrequent settlement days at the fairs."[1] It was also a way of generating money when there was none, or making it appear in a place it had not yet reached, and so lubricating trade if not shaping it on the basis of fictitious assets.

The economic boom in Antwerp in the sixteenth century led financiers to develop management tools that went beyond Venetian methods. The clearinghouse considerably expanded the network of relations for economic actors who were already supranational: transactions were no longer concluded after each deal but closed later on the basis of balances recorded in registers of series of transactions. The already observable linguistic diversity in itself indicates the supranational power conferred by the management of those registers to those in charge of them. Added to this time-bound accounting were certificates of value such as bills of exchange and securities prefiguring our derivatives designed to set prices in advance.

Regardless of the desires of these city-states, high finance took root there. Antwerp, for example, became the financial center of the sixteenth century against its will. The aldermen stayed on the sidelines; "they were even forbidden to have dealings in trade. . . . Foreigners dominated the scene—Hanseatic traders, English, French, and above all southern merchants: Portuguese, Spanish, and Italian."[2] The port of Antwerp was strategically located to distribute Asian and later American products to the markets of northern Europe. But it was also a center that offered no resistance to financial colonization once the local elite had tasted the petty rewards they could secure by making loans.

The state, or the political structures that stood in its place at the time, rather than regulating or even profiting from this nascent capitalist activity, depended on it. Political bodies borrowed capital from those who had it rather than taxing them. Already in Venice, "the Signoria, which had at first been content to levy taxes, began increasingly to resort to loans."[3] Political figures presented themselves to urban stock exchanges as nothing but creditors, like any other merchant conducting business there.

At the turn of the seventeenth century in Amsterdam, the last financial bastion on a municipal scale before the development of national markets, taxation was just as clearly discredited. Fragmented among petty sovereigns, the Netherlands was incapable of intervening. It, too, borrowed from capitalists who settled in the country the funds it did not collect from them in taxes. The regents gradually established ties with the business class, to the point of identifying with it. Hence, the tax system exempted capital and fell only on income and consumption. According to Fernand Braudel, this tax burden perhaps explains the inevitable collapse of Amsterdam: "Indirect taxes, an essential element in a high cost of living, hit the poor hardest. The rich evaded them or could stand the burden better."[4]

Capital became concentrated and so abundant that investments increased their autonomy from strictly commercial activity made up of negotiations and exchanges of goods.

By analogy, one can recognize in the financial bastions of these world economies the characteristic traits of our present-day tax havens: obliteration, disqualification, or ruin of the political elite; absence of taxes; weakness of the role of the state or financing of the state through income tax or indirect taxes borne by wage earners and consumers; internationalization of the financial ruling class; submission of city-states to the vagaries of the market; autonomy of capitalist activity associated with the investment of money; and the identification of power with the fact of owning capital. The methods of financial exploitation that accounts of these city-states report recall contemporary writings by Denis Robert on clearinghouses or the evidence provided by John Christensen on the consequences for the population of Jersey of the transformation of the island into a tax haven.

Hence, it is not surprising that, like the cities that ruled the world economies of the time, tax havens have remained principalities such as Luxembourg, Monaco, and Liechtenstein, specks on the world map, economic entities such as the City of London, or simply cities, such as Halifax and Singapore.

3

THE COLONIAL GENEALOGY OF TAX HAVENS

Nothing so closely resembles a contemporary tax haven as the private Congo, established by King Léopold II of Belgium following the Berlin Conference in 1885. Europe had been dividing up Africa starting from its coasts, but the vast Congolese region had not yet been attributed to any power; only a few trading posts had appeared on the banks of the Congo River. Slavery had officially been abolished in Europe and the notion of the free market was tentatively advancing. Having won a diplomatic gamble, Léopold II, king of the Belgians, established his colony in the Congo on a strictly private basis rather than in the name of the Kingdom of Belgium. By creating a political space dedicated to commerce alone, which depended neither on constitutional formalities nor on the people, Léopold established a new concept of sovereignty, a private and privatized sovereignty in defiance of the peoples of the world, the prototype of the modern tax haven. On this territory, everything would be permitted—including the worst imaginable abuses of the native populations—until shocking accounts of massacres affected European public opinion and Belgium officially took control of the colony in 1908. Yet other sovereign entities of this kind flourish around the world: princely states of little political interest or isolated islands in the Caribbean or elsewhere merchandise their sovereignty in comparable ways, allowing trade to flourish and crime to bear fruit free of the constraints and laws in force in organized states.[1]

The symbol of the island casts an imaginary veil over these instances of colonial exploitation. When Léopold II set about seizing a colony, his breviary was a book by an aptly named lawyer, James William Bayley Money, called *Java, or How to Manage a Colony*. The book lauded the economic virtues of the Dutch system of cultivation on the island of Java and explained how to make a colonial economy profitable. Looking for a utopia like that, at a time when the press was reporting accounts of Stanley in the Congo, Léopold called on him and took advantage of his methods of conquest inspired by the theory of sovereignty. Stanley, like his counterpart Brazza, who acted on a smaller scale on behalf of the French, persuaded local Congo chiefs to sign, without reading them, treaties abdicating all their powers in favor of the newcomers. Just as Europeans recognized the power of the people only when they brought about its abdication, the newcomers recognized the sovereignty of the Congolese people only at the moment they confiscated it. These scraps of paper became pieces of evidence in the diplomatic reception rooms of Europe, notably at the 1885 Berlin Conference. Factitious "transfers of sovereignty" were already at work there to legitimate the appropriation of territory by whites.

It was a period when all sorts of offshore entities were being created even before the term had been coined.

Interests connected to African sovereign entities were strictly private. Territories were handed over to chartered companies, which dealt as they wished with the Congo. Collusion between industrialists and politicians was out in the open. Léopold owned shares in the enterprises that worked in the Congo, while on the coast of East Africa, Emperor Wilhelm II of Germany turned out to be the largest shareholder of the Deutsche Ost-Afrika Gesellschaft, which occupied the concessions. Germany did not make a political decision to colonize the coast of East Africa but turned over to a private association, headed by Carl Peters, the task of conquering territory through agreements, following the models of Stanley and Brazza, so that German companies might prosper there. Germany subsequently transformed Peters's commercial enterprise into a political protectorate. In the course of his conquests, Peters wrote that he wanted "personally to acquire an empire to his taste," comparing himself to the conquerors of Mexico.

The colonization of the global South was carried out precisely through this transformation of public space into a paradise for commerce: Africa signed its surrender at the precise moment that it conformed to the commercial practices of the whites. Stanley himself came to this conclusion when he saw native populations coming to the various trading posts he had opened in the Congo and trade their goods following market processes. "When I saw the terrace plaza being employed as a common market-ground, I became conscious that the victory against aboriginal conservatism was won."[2]

These are the very colonies that now constitute the most formidable tax havens on the planet. Because it was present in Panama, the United States—a former colony that had become a colonialist—was invited to the Paris Colonial Exposition of 1931. The exposition's purpose was to show that colonization was not "an end in itself. It was a moment in history pointing to a distant future when indigenous lands would accede to independence in a community of interest with colonizers."[3] In this respect, Panama was in the vanguard of the transformation of sovereign entities. Less than fifteen years after its accession to independence in 1903, it was possible to register a ship in Panama without being a citizen of the country. The United States had made it an exclusive domain, and Édouard Chambost now calls this free port the "fast food" of tax havens.

But the harmonious utopia of conflict-free sharing between colonizers and colonized is not confirmed by good history books. Rebellions caused the Germans, followed by the English, to gradually abandon the model of the chartered company. This is why this bitter and sometimes violent colonial legacy reverberates today even in the dark humor traditionally exhibited by guides to tax havens. Implicit in colonial rhetoric are the classic figures of the cannibal and the wahine, sharply delineated stereotypes whose origins Roger Boulay has traced to the South Pacific. From the moment in 1768 when Bougainville called the Polynesian Islands heavenly and what is now New Caledonia infernal, words and pictures exploiting that duality have swept through the West. Natives on their exotic islands have thereafter irrevocably been identified as either brutes or nymphs. The island the colonizer came upon was sometimes Dantesque, populated by monstrous eaters of human flesh and festooned with death's heads, and sometimes idyllic, inhabited by luxuriant pleasure lovers who knew nothing of effort because nature itself provided them with everything in abundance. The first kind of island justified the whites' use of strong-arm tactics, the second the degrading prejudices that still justify our sexual tourism today. The colonial esthetic represents "the South Sea Island savage as ugly and cannibalistic, the woman of the islands as beautiful and easy, the islands as infernal or heavenly."[4]

Images of this kind adorn the frontispieces of the Chambost and Duhamel "guides" to tax havens. The one in Duhamel is murky and uncanny (the pronounced incline of the palm trees is evidence of constant gusts of wind) and reflects a fearsome site that the tax explorer will have to conquer to create a world to his liking, whereas the *Guide Chambost* presents a delightful picture: the water reflects American dollar bills somehow glittering in a sunny sky.

And that is only the beginning. The *Guide Chambost* is careful to distinguish natives who are to be classified as cannibals or as wahines. The population of the British Virgin Islands, "80 percent black or mixed-race . . . is much calmer than that of the neighboring American Virgin Islands." Indeed, in the scale of evaluation he applies to each haven to analyze its purpose and characteristics, Édouard Chambost systematically considers questions of "race." He unhesitatingly catalogues them according to a scale of racial value recalling those of Linnaeus and Buffon. In his view, the standard of living, for example, depends on racial questions. He writes, "The population [of Panama] is composed primarily of mixed-race people, 50 percent of Indian origin and 40 percent black, which leaves 10 percent whites, greatly favored from the point of view of wealth compared to their less affluent and darker brothers."[5] Only a mind inclined to racism would find the turn of words amusing. And the author provides a nudge to ease his reader's mind, if necessary.

According to this way of thinking, blacks and Arabs can buy respectability only if they are noble or wealthy. These criteria have the happy result of reducing their numbers, as the author is pleased to see in the case of Monaco: "The population of exotic origin (a very small percentage) is rather well accepted because there are no 'ragheads' but Arab princes, nor 'niggers' but 'gentlemen of color.'" All others are explicitly presented as undesirable. Stopping off in Gibraltar, Chambost takes into account the historical impact of Spaniards, Genoese, Maltese, and North African Jews in the development of the peninsula, and then without missing a beat mentions that to this population "are added 3,800 Moroccans generally employed in construction, under annual contracts, with no immigration for family reunification." These details are intended to be reassuring: the Moroccans are nothing but a workforce entirely under control and limited in its perpetuation.

At the bottom of the ladder are, of course, the natives, taken all together in the chapter on Malaysia. Malaysia

> is theoretically populated by 20 million . . . inhabitants whose origins are 48 percent Malay, 34 percent Chinese, and 9 percent "other," which modestly cloaks hundreds of thousands of aborigines (the only original inhabitants) treated in the same way as their counterparts in America or Australia, as though they had just come down from the coconut tree to join the zoo where "we'd like to exhibit them but we hesitate to confine them there for fear of Amnesty International."

Lurking behind this language is the memory of the colonial exhibitions in which, up until the first third of the twentieth century, Europe exhibited its savages. Elsewhere, Chambost establishes a hierarchy among populations on the basis of language, even within Europe. If Dutch, for example, is charged with being a "barbaric and unpronounceable" language, one can imagine the fate Chambost holds in store for local dialects. Only "folklore enthusiasts" indulge, for example, in the Isle of Man vernacular.

The same witticisms can be found in Grégoire Duhamel. The Chinese, who "listen to Madonna on their Walkman while sipping Coca-Cola," are a happy conquered population; those among them who go looking for a tax haven risk being of no greater value than "a mere tourist from Benin," and money laundering is regrettable only when it benefits Muslim extremists. We are finally made to understand, with false subtlety, that among offshore employees are several "zealous [female] assistants" able to satisfy the unstated expectations of "international leaders over fifty."[6]

We are daily lulled with the rhythm of this esthetic. In themselves, the expressions "tax haven," *"paradis fiscal,"* and *"Steueroasen,"* and "offshore"—like the exotic island that so often represents them—carry a whiff of dark humor. We are captives of these linguistic perversions when today we talk about flags of convenience. This corruption of language inevitably suggests that outlaw jurisdictions are off in the distance, although they also have their seats in the heart of Europe and North America.

As for the emblematic island, now as during the colonial period, it is a screen to divert attention from the trafficking that goes on in accommodating states. In the late nineteenth century, before the Western powers divided up the entire African continent, one of the most coveted points in

Africa was an island, Zanzibar, situated off the east coast.
Trading companies located on the island handled transactions of conquered property and managed colonial affairs,
while on the coast, independent governors of Arabic culture
saw to the smooth conduct of exploitation and plunder, not to
mention the slave trade, which continued at least up to 1873.
The island's location provided access to the coast's resources
without the necessity of confronting the adversity involved in
those harsh conquests, and thereby reduced colonial activity
to a matter of strictly commercial transactions.[7]

In colonial narratives, as in all the guides to tax havens, exotic island tribes do not meet the criteria of civilization because they have dark skin. It is understood that
their customs are reducible to a superstitious art of witch-
craft, that their faith is not solid and can vacillate at any
moment when it confronts the symbols of Western civilization, and that although they are quick to give up everything to enjoy the advantages of Western civilization, they
remain incapable of shedding the underlying darkness that
reappears when the surface is scratched. As Roger Boulay
writes: "The cannibal and the wahine have been civilized,
but deep within them lurks an animal instinct that has never
been definitively tamed, because the civilizing process is supposed to have been at work for too short a time."[8] Similarly,
Bernard Mouralis has shown how easy it is for Westerners
to consider Africans as mad, barbaric beings plunged into
visions that have no contact with concrete reality, forever joy-
ful and magical—another way of saying that they are lazy
and lascivious to a cartoonish degree.[9] Today these colonialist prejudices still shape "scientific" discourse. The elite take
advantage of them to suddenly stigmatize populations acting in tax havens and law-free zones when the time comes to

find scapegoats for the West's problems. Two specialists on the drug trade, Maurice Cusson and Pierre Tremblay, never look in the direction of tax havens or the CIA, as Michael Levine does with brilliance,[10] to understand the operational methods at work in this network. Instead, the two criminologists attempt to explain the phenomenon "upstream" by improvising an anthropology of the uncivilized hinterlands of the drug culture. Downstream in the Western markets, according to them, one finds a multitude of small-scale dealers who don't know each other and are at the mercy of the vagaries of the free market (the magic formula of supply and demand). There are no bridgeheads, leaders, or orchestrators of the networks. It is only upstream that communities are organized and plots are fomented, in "a territory where the drugs produced have been cultivated for a long time and where their consumption has been integrated into village social life, having been sanctioned by custom and habit." Following the authors' argument, it becomes clear why they make these distant countries the source of the problem: "It is also necessary that there be a peasant mass with sufficient skill, that it be poor, and that it depend on these crops to survive. Such a labor force is not to be found in the West, but several regions in the Third World satisfy these conditions."[11] This is a scientific and sanitary way of cleansing the West. A tradition of colonialist knowledge supports the falsification and defies rationality to come to the conclusion that the alleged moral backwardness, moral destitution, and moral inferiority of those lands are corrupting the spotlessly innocent West, which is strictly focused on peaceful commerce between civilized nations.

4

THE CREATION OF MODERN TAX HAVENS

Capitalism developed in the nineteenth century in conjunction with the concepts of political sovereignty and the prerogatives of nation-states. Trade was strictly regulated by the rules in force in sovereign states under their legal systems. State sovereignty divided and codified national spaces in order to ensure their oversight of questions of responsibility and then to induce all physical or formally constituted social actors to take their places in one of those sovereign spaces to give their activity a legal basis. In light of the internationalization of exchanges, the proliferation of sovereign spaces opened the way to competition between states to attract great global investors by offering them the best conditions.[1]

This competitive system originated in the crisis of the state inaugurated by the signature of the Treaty of Westphalia in 1648 that ended the Thirty Years' War. This treaty established for the long term—through laws, institutions, and rules—the terms of territorial control by which the state was defined. But more than that, for the signatory

powers it marked the interruption of a teleological design
and a historical dynamic that had until then seemed to dictate their destiny. Michel Foucault offers this analysis: "The
old forms of universality offered to and imposed on Europe"
disappeared; "the Empire is not the ultimate vocation of all
states." The reality principle led states to consider their interests according to the competitive relations that defined
them. Evidence of this is provided by the notion of reason of
state, and its corollary, state secrets, according to which the
supreme institutional authority authorized itself to overcome
its own laws and to conduct itself, in contingent historical
rivalries, less according to its constitution than according to
an art that gave intuition and the idea of political genius
more than their due. It was not "laws, a constitution, or even
the virtue of magistrates" that were at work.[2] The state conducted itself less according to principles, a morality, and an
ideal of divine inspiration than according to techniques,
data, and applied knowledge. Demography became essential,
as did the mastery of agricultural possibilities and an inven-
tory of animals. Maps of natural resources began to appear.
Sociological pictures of the population were sketched.

Every state had its protégés in an international market
that was opening up to competition. This competitive spirit
gradually extended its influence to the tax question itself: in
the 1880s in the United States, New Jersey and Delaware offered tax exemptions to large companies in order to attract
them, thereby establishing a national and eventually global
race to the bottom in matters of taxation. Many years later,
in 1981, banks were again invited to move to Delaware.

This tax competition and the growth of multinational
companies created legal confusion about tax issues. What
should happen, for example, when a company incorporated

in one country operates through subsidiaries in another? Christian Chavagneux and Ronen Palan write, "Two principles seem to be non-negotiable: the principle of the exclusive sovereignty of each state on its territory and the principle of the support of the major industrialized countries . . . for their leading companies and their internationalization."[3]

These were the circumstances in which jurists, diplomats, and politicians knitted together an international or multilateral commercial law enabling sovereign powers to determine among themselves the articles, decisions, and traditions that would prevail, depending on the matter in dispute. Chavagneux and Palan have shown how, in the interstices between their different national laws, states themselves developed decision-making bodies controlled directly by financial actors. Once they had guaranteed mutual protection of foreign investors on their territory (the Anglo-French Cobden-Chevalier Treaty), because the powers of states were limited to their prerogatives on their respective territories, they were unable to control taxation. States usually turned over to economic actors the task of organizing international law and organizations to regulate methods of exchange involving them (as their exclusive property even though the social activity of whole populations depended on these arrangements). This "permitted the growth of a branch of international law, *lex mercatoria*, the law of merchants, whose practices originated in the Middle Ages."[4]

Moreover, British courts issued two decisions on the right to tax that set a precedent and established the political legitimacy of tax havens. They unwittingly gave legal legitimacy to the principle of the fictitious incorporation of companies in accommodating jurisdictions. The legal question raised in 1876 was where a British company operating

in India and Italy should pay its taxes. The court determined
that it should pay its taxes in the United Kingdom, the location of its registered office. The principle was confirmed in
1906 in the case of the De Beers Company, which exploited
diamond mines in South Africa. Because it was resident in
England, that was where it must pay taxes. This principle was
manipulated: by registering its head office or a subsidiary
managing one or another sector of activity in an accommodating jurisdiction, a company could shelter itself from tax.

The search was on for any exotic location or British
principality, about which history is full of anecdotes, to justify tax rates of practically zero: residents of the Cayman
Islands were freed from all taxation by George III after their
1798 rescue from shipwreck of a group of English nobles and
officials sailing off their coast. The pursuit of pirates in the
Caribbean lay behind the formal establishment of trade in
the islands of the region; Canadian banks laid the basis for
the bulk of the banking activity in those offshore centers. In
1765, the British crown purchased the Isle of Man from the
duke of Atholl to put an end to smuggling. Monaco abolished
its taxes in 1868 to make its casino more attractive. The port
region of Hong Kong, a British dependency until 1997, developed its banking sector, chiefly around the gold market,
secured access (in neighboring China and at prices defying
any competition) to the raw materials needed by the textile
industry, and instituted the first major foreign-trade zone in
the modern world to manufacture consumer goods.

In a second phase, advocates of offshore activity found
political and legal resources within the jurisdictions that had
accommodated them to carry on activities that were prohib-
ited in their countries of origin. Offshore, one turned out
to be impregnable, especially when "bank secrecy" was re-

inforced, as in Switzerland in 1934. Switzerland established criminal penalties for any disclosure of information to a third party by an employee in the banking sector. Several tax havens, particularly in the Caribbean, adopted Swiss law and thereby made it impossible for foreign judges concerned with white-collar crime to conduct any investigations.

During World War II, Switzerland consolidated its position as a tax haven because its status as a neutral territory enabled citizens of countries at war with each other to sign trade agreements. Bank secrecy covered Chase Bank, Coca-Cola, IBM, and Standard Oil, as well as Prescott Bush and gold and diamond traffickers doing business with the Germans.

In the late 1950s and early 1960s, the City of London gradually developed the Eurodollar market in a totally opaque manner.

By perverting certain international measures two legal systems were linked together: the system of traditional states and its negative double, the tax haven system made to order to favor capital flight. This is exemplified in international treaties against double taxation, designed so that companies, present in the form of subsidiaries in jurisdictions other than that of their residence, might avoid paying taxes on identical sums in two places. In the 1920s, the League of Nations formalized these agreements usually enabling companies to evade taxation.[5] There is in fact a kind of tax shopping at work with regard to inheritance taxes and individual and corporate income taxes. By virtue of the principle that the same income is not taxed twice in different jurisdictions, the interested parties try to establish their domicile where the tax rate is the most advantageous and then repatriate their capital without being taxed again. The treaties barring

double taxation soon became treaties for double nontaxa-
tion, in the quip made by Jean Merckaert of CCFD–Terre
Solidaire.[6]

States remained active in shaping the economy for only
a few decades during the second half of the century, enough
time to heal the wounds of the worldwide war, to recover from
the still raw memory of the economic dislocations of 1929,
and to establish a competitive balance of power. Capitalist
states established themselves as arbiters at the intersection
of industrial and financial capital owned by shareholders
benefiting from the postwar economic recovery with wage
earners conscious of historical class relations.

The second half of the twentieth century signaled above all
the advent of electronic finance and autonomous capital that
together created the "financial planet." Financial actors had
ever greater means to keep the state at bay and to endow
their interests with a sovereignty that outpaced that of the
state. The advent of sophisticated techniques of finance cou-
pled with the historical contingencies of the second half of
the twentieth century gave finance the appearance of being
a world government. The first havens of a commerce freed
from any political constraints—the commercial ports of
the Renaissance—reappeared in history with ever greater
intensity.

In *Un monde sans loi*, Jean de Maillard points out how
the uncontrolled development of the monetary economy of
the United States helped to free world finance from all political oversight, enabling it to set itself up as a sovereign
historical force. In the 1960s, borrowing was encouraged
at the same time that inflation facilitated the repayment of
loans; "debtors, taking advantage of inflation, were even able

to benefit from negative interest rates, rates lower than the rate of inflation."[7] Postwar reconstruction also encouraged American dollar investments overseas; it became practically impossible for states to contain economic development within their own borders. At the slightest disturbance, when shareholders lost money or were unsatisfied with the results of their investments, capital made use of competition by investing in places where pressure could be put on wages and the costs of taxation could be reduced. As far as taxation and professional regulation were concerned, the state found itself powerless when it tried to tax capital to finance programs in the public interest that were its responsibility. Capital transcended mere national boundaries and concentrated in a higher global stratum. Washington, which supplied the world with currency, feared that the United States domestic market would suffer the inflationary shocks of a monetary surplus, and so it encouraged American companies to reinvest these financial gains in foreign countries, particularly in Europe. Eurodollars and petrodollars thus made their appearance—the profits from American dollar investments that the authorities in Washington wanted to keep away from their territory. A new large-scale tax haven in the banking sector then developed in the heart of Europe, in the City of London. The British financial elite sensed the opportunity and imposed itself "as the prime international financial center in 1957 by opening the way to contemporary offshore finance by creating Eurodollar markets," write Chavagneux and Palan.[8] The opening of international exchange markets in 1958 enabled London to conduct a considerable number of the world's foreign exchange transactions and to profit from the crisis of confidence affecting the American dollar. This offshore market, developed primarily by the most powerful states, exhibited once again the most frequently denounced characteristics: practically tax-free capital, bank secrecy, and lack of cooperation with international justice. By abruptly ending the parity between the dollar and gold in 1971, President Nixon promoted an entire speculative sector focused on the currency exchange markets. Chavagneux and Palan explain:

> Financiers realized that the constraints of the 1950s and 1960s had no purchase on capital held outside its home territory. . . . Once finance was able by itself to ensure the financing of the economy outside the control of any administration, banks and financial establishments found themselves in a position of strength. Creditors had recovered their rights against debtors. . . . The creditor was in a position of strength to extract the maximum profit from the debtor for the money he had provided.

Unable to maintain access to credit as readily as before, to protect their labor forces from relocation, international subcontracting, and the automation of labor, one by one states deregulated their economies to attract "nomadic capital" that they had no power to tax. The states put themselves at the service of capital and negotiated large free-trade agreements on its behalf that arranged the global arena in which capital could circulate unconstrained. International institutions such as the World Bank and the International Monetary Fund established the rules wherever there was a need for foreign capital. Finance became the master of the game, although it was not attached to any state. Hence, actors in all social categories turned to financiers: states in the

North borrowed the capital they no longer had to finance the services that they provided less and less successfully; states in the South borrowed funds to finance the very debt that was already burdening them; companies sought to attract them for their development, and individuals for housing and retirement pensions. "At every level the economy depends on speculative capital, because widespread deregulation has made instability permanent," state Chavagneux and Palan.[9]

Tax havens merely radicalized this logic. International capital finds in them an anchorage with no constraints. It feels at home. These European principalities and other microstates, once marginal, are completely fitting for its new autonomy. They turn themselves into money states and give actors registered in this special international stratum the political base they need to make them politically sovereign. Chavagneux and Palan write, "The birth of the Eurodollar market in the late 1950s marked the first step in the period of financial globalization that we know today: allowing offshore capital to circulate without public control. It was by becoming central actors in the Eurodollar markets that tax havens were able to acquire the predominant position they occupy today."[10] Tax havens became opportune blind spots where different funds could be mingled and any representative of the public who ventured to investigate their origin could be confounded.

5

CRIMINAL LAIRS

It goes without saying that the development of this sovereignty of finance released from the constraints of the rule of law was a godsend for organized crime, drug cartels, and organizations with questionable aims. The lawless world of finance that opened up for them made possible not only an exponential growth of their activities on an international scale but also a mingling of their funds with the funds of legitimate activities still governed by the rule of law, so it was no longer possible to distinguish between money from crime and money circulating according to legal rules.

Mafia organizations, still represented in a violent light in the cinema, have in places grown considerably more civilized since they have begun to act without making any more noise than the clicking of their laptops. This evolution in Italy has been described in the Weber-inspired work of the anthropologist Pino Arlacchi on "the Mafia ethic and the spirit of capitalism."[1] After brutally establishing themselves in the late nineteenth century, the Mafia clans and crime

syndicates maintained their hold on regional industries in
the early twentieth, while also guaranteeing a degree of order in the regions they occupied. This went so far that the
state conceded some of its power to them—for example, by
turning over to some of their elements the functions of regional administrators. The Mafia protected those who served
it, intervened more successfully than the state was able to as
a mediator in conflicts, and if necessary imposed repressive
measures. But this is far distant from the code of honor that
novelists under the spell of the shady world have wrongly attributed to criminal circles.[2] The Mafia was, on the contrary,
made for the offshore world, in which no code substitutes for
a constitutional framework that would make this authority
morally predictable and would operationally govern the exercise of its power. Violence and arbitrariness are the rule
and no convention really has a place. The "men of honor"
hold undivided rule over the local society and act as intermediaries with foreign merchants, particularly in the trade of
agricultural products and alcoholic beverages.

At the end of World War II, a major demographic exodus caused by mass unemployment affected the regions the
Mafia controlled, principally Calabria and Sicily. The central
government took advantage of this "great transformation"
to once again assert its rights. Provincial leaders were rel-
egated to the rank of mere hoodlums, but this regression ac-
celerated the conversion of the Mafia to the world of finance.
It was a matter of asserting control not so much over territory as over financial capital. Practicing a particular form
of entryism, various Mafia networks learned how to distract
the nascent regional bureaucracy of the modernized Italian
state from its purposes. Then, using their customary violent
methods, yesterday's hoodlums swiftly raised themselves

into the ranks of respectable businessmen by accomplishing a "primitive accumulation" of capital that it would have been impossible to generate with legal methods: they intimidated suppliers, physically attacked their competitors, occupied by force the key spaces of production, diversified their monopoly power (stock breeding, industry, tourism), put pressure on the wages of their employees, scoffed at social security and insurance payments, did not acknowledge their personnel's overtime, and regularly violated contracts.

On the basis of such practices, Mafia leaders were able to make a place for themselves in business. For example, a billion-lire ransom paid in 1973 constituted the initial investment in a monopoly of road transportation. Unfair competition produced colossal advantages. At the same time as the financial Mafia secured access to funds from varieties of illegal trafficking and to capital held by banks tied to crime, it positioned itself among the financial elite acting completely legally in law-governed states. The two most powerful networks in Calabria in the 1970s, for example, controlled monopolies in many strategic sectors, while simultaneously participating in other networks. One of them had "a monopoly of the olive and citrus trade in three communes: the profits its members ha[d] made from drug-trafficking, jewel-smuggling, robbery and extortion have been invested in building a string of modern olive-processing factories," writes Pino Arlacchio. Legalized, this production later benefited from European Union subsidies. Foreign private companies, such as Coca-Cola, tried to come to terms with Italian Mafia powers to take advantage of this exceptionally profitable investment framework. Once its industrial, financial, and criminal empire had been established, the Mafia network transformed itself sociologically into a reputed industrial and financial company and recruited into its ranks lawyers, tax experts, and legal technicians. There then came on the scene "the 'counsellor,' the lawyer who is part of the mafia's inner circle," reports Arlacchi.[3]

But Italy nonetheless was not transformed into a lawless world. One obstacle remained: the judiciary, an institution relatively independent from the political authorities. And when it fell to the justice system to publicly get to the bottom of things, it was not so much to distinguish criminals from legal wheeler-dealers as to report the total interconnection between the criminal and legal economies. The legitimate and Mafia economies of Italy found they had a common purpose, and so they became intermingled. As Arlacchi notes, "an unwonted 'hitch' in the course of justice—due, perhaps, to the excessive zeal of an investigator, a judge's unusual 'rigidity,' or the stubbornness of a witness—may decide the course of an entrepreneur's career, or upset a dominant position in the heroin business, and this may lead in turn to the loss of tens of thousands of millions of lire, the failure of a string of companies, and the sacking of numerous employees."[4]

It is at that point that tax havens became interesting for criminal actors converted to finance. They preserved what Arlacchi calls the "sovereignty" of Mafia groups. They had to register outside the reach of judges the illicit aspects of their business activities, while maintaining an honest façade in Italy to enable them to launder and invest the proceeds of crime. The Mafia reverted to very old methods in tax havens, like the "mille-feuille" technique. In the past this meant depositing funds from illegal trafficking in the accounts of actual laundries with no customers. Because the volumes were much greater this time, it was no longer small businesses but large import-export companies, airlines, and supermarket chains that made it possible to mingle criminal and legitimate revenues. And to escape from the constraints of the rule of law, Mafia sovereignties looked toward tax havens, in particular Switzerland. Pino Arlacchi ends his book by pointing at an offshore horizon. Roberto Saviano in a sense picks up the thread by reporting on how Mafia dealings in Campania now develop offshore. The violent businessmen of the region of Caserta were behind huge commercial frauds involving the Cirio and Parmalat companies.

Marie-Christine Dupuis-Danon, who once worked for the anti-money-laundering unit of the UN, has analyzed this phenomenon on a global scale. About these criminal organizations, which are increasingly difficult to identify and indict, she writes that "they have diversified their investments to orient themselves toward legitimate activities that earn them respectability, may serve as cover for new trafficking or the laundering of dirty money, and incidentally generate new capital to increase their already substantial wealth."[5] It has consequently become difficult to distinguish a legal action from another that is not, because tax havens make it possible to legalize actions that are considered illicit under the rule of law. These networks are to be found in almost every region of the world. Investors who owe to crime the primitive accumulation of their capital may come from the drug circuits that ramify from the Caribbean to Europe and America, or may be corrupt African heads of state supported by the West and by international institutions, when they are not Latin American coca producers or Southeast Asian heroin producers. And, of course, the yakuzas (Japanese gangs) and the powerful Russian mob should not be forgotten.

In this way the proceeds of crime are largely reinvested in the traditional economic market and have asserted themselves as key sources of financing. States that today are trying so hard to attract this capital in the form of "foreign investment" to create jobs and benefit their economy have lost all their scruples. Tax havens offer discretion and the services required to transform criminal funds into coveted assets in market economies. "The considerable growth of banking havens and offshore companies has been parallel to the increase in fictitious activities justified exclusively by the need to conceal dirty money. Why were these criminal havens allowed to proliferate? Because covert finance has all the appearances of true finance. It shares the same circuits and meets the same requirements of solvency and credit," writes Jean de Maillard.[6]

Hence, nothing distinguishes with certainty funds drawn from illegal arms sales and those drawn from mining, the fruits of political corruption from the profits from retail gasoline sales. Through countless ramifications, money circulates in every direction; legitimate money finances activities that are not, and criminal activities support the growth of market economies formally operating under the rule of law.

Today, the companies that have adopted this kind of maneuver are well established, and the documents that exist about them set out financial arrangements of breathtaking complexity: evidence was presented that the oil company Elf massively participated in arms trafficking in Angola at the same time that it was selling gasoline to French consumers;[7] that Air America, secretly owned by the CIA, permitted drug trafficking on aircraft transporting civilians;[8] that the French beverage company Ricard profited from laundering Colombian cocaine revenues;[9] and that the Canadian Imperial Bank of Commerce managed the Swiss bank accounts of the dictator Omar Bongo's bodyguards along with those of honest Canadian investors.[10]

Judge Eva Joly estimates that half the forty largest financial institutions in Paris "operate in markets where repeated instances of corruption, secret commissions, and kickbacks have been observed and acknowledged by the principal intermediaries," and that "half of very large French companies are directly confronted every day with financial criminality."[11]

Consider the Parmalat case. In the fall of 2003, it was discovered that the company had been concealing enormous liabilities of nearly €15 billion, primarily in accounts in Luxembourg controlled by Citibank. As *Le Monde* pointed out, Parmalat was an empire that specialized in financial speculation and offshore transactions which, incidentally, produce[d] milk and yogurt."[12] The Italian company had issued bonds from its Luxembourg hub, recurrent public debt instruments that were particularly suspect because the company claimed to be very profitable. The €7.5 billion provided by investors disappeared from the company's offshore accounts, sometimes empty shells, sometimes forgotten setups that showed nothing but losses. Dazzling amounts were misappropriated in this way, while others were probably laundered by going through the Cayman Islands. When the company imploded, Parmalat's debt amounted to ten times its assets. One billion euros was found in an account in Monaco.[13] Accounting manipulations involving derivatives were also used to dupe the least initiated among investors.

It remains very difficult to measure the magnitude of the problem with any precision. Daily financial transactions around the globe are now calculated in trillions of dollars. Half the world's money supply moves through or resides in tax havens. This means that colossal volumes of exchanges are conducted outside the control of legitimate governments. It is almost impossible for the human mind to grasp their scope, and all attempts to enable us to master data of such magnitude are of little help. For example, when Sylvain Besson describes the assets of Swiss banks with the image of a swimming pool three football fields long, 70 yards wide, and 13 yards deep, filled with Swiss twenty-franc notes,[14] it brings to mind these lines by Mallarmé:

> I have some notion of what sums might be, by the hundreds and beyond, equal to those whose enunciation in the closing arguments during a trial involving high finance, leave one cold as far as their existence is concerned. The inability of grandiloquent figures to express anything is a special case; one finds, by this measure, that if a number increases and moves in the direction of the improbable, it contains more zeros, meaning that its total is spiritually equivalent to nothing, almost.[15]

In the view of François Morin, former member of the board of directors of the Banque de France, data such as these "no longer make sense" to common mortals, nor to financial analysts, government authorities, or any economic decision maker. "Not only has the loss of meaning grown deeper every day for citizens of planet Earth, but the lack of understanding and adaptability on the part of the major governmental authorities in the world continues to provoke anxiety in light of the very concrete dangers and challenges posed by financial globalization," writes Morin.[16]

But the available evaluations of offshore criminality are

staggering. In 2005, Raymond W. Baker, a Harvard graduate, a businessman in Africa, and a consultant, put to the test the estimate IMF director Michel Camdessus had made in 1998 that between 2 and 5 percent of the world gross domestic product (between $640 billion and $1.6 trillion annually) derived from money-laundering operations. By broadening the definition to the problem of tax evasion and by also considering money-laundering operations within national borders, Baker estimates the annual total to be at least $1 trillion. That includes the traffic in drugs and arms, the markets for counterfeit goods and counterfeit currency, human trafficking, and various other rackets. This total also includes the sums at stake in influence peddling and corruption as well as, in the commercial realm, the sums from tax evasion, the proceeds of accounting manipulation and falsification, and price transfers (transactions a company does with itself so as to register profits in tax-free jurisdictions).[17] This estimate covers only laundered money, transfers of funds from secret budgets to publicly declared budgets in law-governed jurisdictions. The annual global criminal budget is estimated at $1.5 trillion.

According to Merrill Lynch/Cap Gemini Ernst & Young, individuals holding assets of $1 million or more in tax havens have collectively deposited $8.5 trillion in them. The Boston Consulting Group reaches an estimate of $38 trillion when it considers the fortunes of individuals annually investing more than $250,000 offshore. To that should be added the funds invested in even greater quantities by multinational companies and corrupt heads of state.

All these data should be considered with some reservation. They are in fact underestimates if one considers, independently of statistical data, that money invested in tax havens funds shameful projects on a massive scale. In off-shore sovereign entities capital can support illegal or even openly criminal trafficking without necessarily being laundered by the machinery and the subterfuges imagined by financial engineering. This capital is added to laundered capital to be reinvested in the real economy.

The economist Éric Vernier is baffled by the magnitude of the criminal economy that has grown up offshore. He subscribes to the estimate that the annual gross criminal product (GCP) is $1.5 trillion: "Well, $1.5 trillion—it doesn't matter that I'm a financier; after a few zeros I have trouble seeing how much that makes. And if one compares it to the richest countries, the empire of crime or the kingdom of crime should be invited to join the G8, because it is the eighth largest world power."[18] Moreover, $4.5 trillion of "gray money" circulates through these same channels, the proceeds of financial crime, fraudulent accounting operations, and embezzlement.

The most profitable of these criminal networks is the drug network, with an annual GCP of $1 trillion, which places it second among all worldwide commercial activities, whether criminal or legal. But other networks are very profitable: Vernier mentions the sex industry and prostitution, pedophilia, the traffic in human organs, counterfeiting (particularly of medicines), and waste treatment.

The international banking system is very well lubricated. With respect to its architecture, the journalist Denis Robert questions the dynamic role played by the international "settlement" mechanisms Clearstream and Euroclear, both situated in jurisdictions that provide banking secrecy (respectively, Luxembourg and Belgium). These supernotaries of world financial activity manage a kind of "black box" of high finance: they record international banking transactions like a world-scale private firm of notaries. "The firm dematerializes securities and records them in the form of numbers. All securities: shares of stock, Treasury bills, bonds," writes Robert.[19] In their book *Révélation$*, Robert and Ernest Backes write: "Even though Euroclear is located in Belgium, it is nonetheless an American creation, set up by Morgan Guaranty Trust Company of New York in December 1968. Worried by the control of a single entity over such a powerful financial instrument, a group of 66 banks, including, for example Chase Manhattan Bank of New York, established the firm Cedel in Luxembourg in September 1970, which later became Clearstream."[20] The international transactions recorded by these settlement companies are inaccessible to investigators or to judges of individual countries; banking secrecy protects them legally and sophisticated forms of coding protects them technically. Ten years ago, Clearstream recorded annual transactions on the order of $65 trillion. Denis Robert describes it as the banks' own offshore banker. In their study of the "black boxes" of finance, Denis Robert and Ernest Backes assert that funds can move from one bank account to another without appearing in the public accounts of the organization, thereby permitting, under cover of the most airtight secrecy, illicit and criminal transfers of money or securities.[21] One hundred countries are involved in this financial sophistication, forty of which are offshore microstates or European tax and banking havens, including the Bahamas, Andorra, Bahrain, Barbados, the Cayman Islands, China, the Cook Islands, Guernsey, Hong Kong, Ireland, Monaco, Panama, Singapore, Switzerland, and Taiwan.[22] But these states have no geopolitical relevance; they are names on lists that make it possible, through accounting manipulations and legal acrobatics, to evade the rules governing legitimate states. Robert writes:

> Tax havens are mirages, ghost towns at the end of the runway. It is futile to search in them for what you will not find. Financial vehicles have in a sense simulated a deposit there. The financial information remains recorded and accessible in the electronic archives of the transfer stations of a capitalism that is growing increasingly clandestine. It is always Clearstream and Euroclear. The former has its headquarters in a tax haven, Luxembourg, a place where an independent judge will never set foot. We seem to have come full circle.[23]

It therefore appears plausible that an oil company can practice corruption or mobilize mercenaries in a state in crisis without the money involved being formally recorded among its international transactions. We know that Clearstream spared no effort to have the courts declare "defamatory" that logical deduction, reached on the basis of information that the journalist had gathered. As a consequence, the media dared to cover the activities of this settlement center only in the treatment of a peripheral "Clearstream affair," a judicial melodrama opposing two leaders of the French political elite around the use of lists attributed to that institution, this time falsified; that use might have affected the political career of one of the protagonists. But for a public historically subjected to the effects of the instantaneous and secret exchange of potentially criminal securities and funds, the real use of the genuine lists would have been of much more interest than this media-judicial circus.

The panoply of methods used by the technicians of money laundering that Baker describes in his book clearly gives evidence of how difficult it is to measure the magnitude of the phenomenon with any rigor. Improper billing to finance secret commissions in public contracts leaves absolutely no trace. Price transfers, whereby a company sells its own product to itself at cost through its subsidiaries located in tax havens, mean that its profit is recorded in its offshore accounts, where it is subject to little or no taxation. More than half of all intracompany exchanges involve this kind of operation. False insurance payments on alleged production defects are even better concealed: "everything is decided in advance and covered by the original purchase price." To this may be added fake lawsuits, transfers of funds from hidden circuits to legal networks with no apparent connection between the two, false winnings from casinos, the concealment of dirty money in stock exchange transactions, and false loans secured by dirty money through a myriad of offshore shell corporations.[24]

A question also arises about the category to which one should ascribe the part played by the many service providers required for finance's dirty work. "What are we talking about," wonders Jean de Maillard,

> when, to challenge or confirm their existence, we talk of the hundreds of billions of dollars allocated to drug trafficking? And where does the counting of assets stop? Are we talking about the street resale market or the revenues of criminal organizations? Should we also include in the calculation the laundering of drug money, and all the legal and financial engineering busy giving it all the appearances of legitimacy? Bankers,

lawyers, notaries, real estate agents, stockbrokers, accountants, and many other professionals contribute, not always innocently, to the operation of the criminal economy. They don't even need to hide because they are merely doing their jobs, sometimes simply by closing their eyes.[25]

These reflections on the way offshore evil has become commonplace suggest that the estimate of criminal funds involved should be multiplied to an immeasurable degree.[26]

The question of tax breaks given by the countries of the North also remains open. Tax evasion based on offshore havens has proliferated in legitimate states and enables many multinationals headquartered there to pay no income at the end of the tax year.

Furthermore, statistical and accounting data from the South are much less reliable than those, still far from perfect, from the bureaucratized states of the North. Baker was the first to point to economies with "the weakest legal structures," which "facilitates unrecorded economic activity."[27] In his documentary *Katanga Business*, Thierry Michel shows that in a single day, the customs officers in Katanga were able to collect $20 million in custom duties when Governor Moïse Katumbi suddenly ordered that controls be enforced.[28] The flows of dirty money are unfathomable, without even mentioning the questionable use made in many jurisdictions of the diplomatic pouch. Indeed, according to R.T. Naylor, the black market in gold operates at every stage of the mining of and trade in the precious metal.[29] This unrecorded flow of money from corruption, criminal trafficking, or white-collar crime is, according to Baker, "the biggest loophole in the free-market system," and the most harmful to the disadvantaged. The economic crime that has the greatest historical consequences is also the one that is the hardest to measure.

Available accounting estimates are rough guesses because no public body with research resources adequate to the magnitude of the task has ever seriously tried to thoroughly document the financial flows that escape the control of legitimate governments. "There is no place in international financial statistics for 'dirty money' or 'laundered proceeds' or 'flight capital' or 'trade mispricing' or any account remotely suggesting such figures. Most illicit flows are either disguised or invisible . . . therefore hard data are nonexistent," writes Baker.[30] These data might bring to light the deep entanglement between the proceeds of crime and the "legitimate" economy of the West. Worse, they would show that Western banks and governments attract this illicit capital for their own benefit and that public decision makers in the North turn out to be accomplices in many activities that can reasonably be characterized as criminal. They would therefore show that offshore international finance has not only unknowingly received assets from criminal networks that had learned how to use the instruments of the market but also grown exponentially by joining its interests to others that are open to serious challenge.

Criminal activity and the practically absolute deregulation of international financial controls (opening the foreign exchange markets to all comers, securitization of various debts, derivatives based in real assets) explain concomitantly the exponential growth of offshore organizations and offshore power.

The banking secrecy that prevails in tax havens and secrecy jurisdictions makes it possible to conceal transactions with business partners of any kind, as well as the identities

of holders of bank accounts, company directors, or trust beneficiaries, as well as the sums of money involved in the operations in question. Wealthy individuals and private companies
that have access to tax havens also enjoy tax and judicial
provisions developed in their favor. Tax havens have given
body to a once generous-minded slogan: it is forbidden to
forbid.

6

A PERFECT UNION
BETWEEN LEGITIMATE STATES AND TAX HAVENS

The order of magnitude of offshore transactions has turned out to be absolutely staggering and raises the questions of responsibility and oversight to an unimagined degree. These exchanges are not confined to nest eggs put in tax shelters, but come from funds that work outside any legal framework. Either this money feeds illicit circuits whose purpose is to pillage the resources of the South whose economies are immersed in criminality or, laundered in tax havens, the money generates funds that enable "investors" enjoying unfair advantages to play a major role in the economies of the North.

Legitimate states facilitate this conflation of private funds from different sources by not forcing companies to present balance sheets distinguishing among their various components. The former judge and current European deputy Eva Joly is offended by this. The overall profits presented by multinationals and other companies in the form of "consolidated balance sheets" make it impossible to learn what use they make of tax havens. Joly writes, "Currently, companies publish only consolidated accounts. As a result, we know, for example, that Total had nearly €13 billion in profits last year, but we don't know where. If this information was published, we would see that it earns significant profits in Mauritius and Bermuda and very little in Algeria or Angola."[1] Today, even supporters of the capitalist system are frankly worried: "Tax havens and secrecy jurisdictions permit operations outside the law and outside the process of regulation. This benefits the generators and facilitators of criminal, corrupt, and commercial dirty money far more than it benefits the legitimate capitalist system," writes Raymond W. Baker.[2]

That said, even when they are aware of the problem, reputedly legitimate states seem to strive to make these machinations ever more efficient. Think of the highly criticized offshore jurisdictions in the Caribbean. The worm was in the fruit from the very beginning. In the nineteenth and twentieth centuries, banks that set up shop in the islands were already participating in projects incompatible with the principles of the rule of law. Taking advantage of the commercial relations Governor Jean Talon had established between New France and the French West Indies, two Nova Scotia banks, Merchants' Bank (now the Royal Bank of Canada) and the Bank of Nova Scotia (now Scotiabank), gradually developed a network of branches in the Caribbean islands. But when local competition eroded Canadian business, this liberal manifestation of the free-market economy nonetheless benefited from a providential boost sponsored by the Ottawa government. In these circumstances, Canada sent its army to the Caribbean.[3] In 1837, London threw its weight onto the scale; the center of British banking activity in the Caribbean dependencies, the Colonial Bank, gave Canadian institutions a banking monopoly.

Acting first as a link between the neighboring United States and the United Kingdom, in the twentieth century Canadian banks in the Caribbean developed a panoply of services that served any interest requiring offshore discretion. They held a wide majority position there throughout the century. And they were not noticed until the 1970s, when an affair arose that had repercussions in the United States. In a report filed in Washington, Senate investigators wrote that in the Caribbean "a major Canadian international bank has a consistent reputation for encouraging dirty money."[4] At the same time, the Bank of Nova Scotia was caught up in a legal storm.

The investigation by Mario Possamai, *Money on the Run: Canada and How the World's Profits Are Laundered*, is a landmark study. Among others, it quotes Rod Stamler, former assistant commissioner of the Royal Canadian Mounted Police, who says that through techniques of money laundering, high-level criminal connections have been established between Canadians and foreigners in the Caribbean: "There are so many ways of transferring money during a commercial transaction that it's virtually impossible to distinguish between what is the legitimate money and what is the illegal money." In the 1980s, a convicted American drug dealer, Robert Twist, explained in detail on Canadian public television how he deposited a considerable sum in installments in a Canadian bank in the Caribbean without ever being questioned.[5]

Competition in banking in the Caribbean did not really make itself felt until 1981, when the Federal Reserve System authorized New York financial institutions, and subsequently others throughout the United States, to operate directly in tax havens, precisely so they could avoid the inconveniences of national legislation without having to leave the country.[6] Because it was from the Caribbean that American banks granted loans to Western countries with liquidity shortages, the nations of the North became further subordinate to offshore interests. Through this initiative, moreover, the economically ultraliberal Reagan regime hoped eventually to force the deregulation of international banking, so as to facilitate the access of American banks to other countries of the North. Through this measure, the American authorities claimed they would be in a better position to control money laundering, which a Senate investigation had estimated at $75 billion annually.

But obviously the opposite happened. The Cayman Islands, which had two banks on its territory in 1964, counted no fewer than 450 in 1983, in addition to more than 270 insurance firms and 14,000 other companies that had popped up—more institutions than residents in the archipelago. Robert T. Naylor, an economist at McGill University, is at a loss to find any logical reason that can justify the paradoxical position adopted by the International Monetary Fund (IMF) in those years to support the Cayman Islands financially so they would be able to establish banking and financial infrastructures that facilitated tax evasion, corruption, and capital flight from the countries of the South, the same capital that the IMF had loaned to those countries under pressure because of their budget deficits.

Alex Doulis, the high priest of tax evasion in Canada, explains in *My Blue Haven*, his manual tinged with dark humor, that the Caribbean tax havens have advantages over the European principalities because they were developed from scratch as tax havens and secrecy jurisdictions, in the

manner of an ideal type, and not because of historical acci-
dent, as was true of their European counterparts. Legitimate
states do share responsibility for this Caribbean master-
piece. Among the some eighty offshore jurisdictions in the
world, competition has necessarily developed in a race to the
bottom. The various tax havens in the Caribbean, already
at the geographical heart of a flourishing drug traffic from
Colombia, have gradually extended their range of services
to embody the generic sense of tax haven. Foreign-trade
zones, free ports, and flags of convenience; bank secrecy and
numbered accounts; branches of the world's major banks
and financial expertise; newly established banks, trusts, and
holding companies; tax-exempt and offshore corporations,
foundations, and insurance companies; treaties on double
taxation with various legitimate states around the world—
nothing seems to have been forgotten.

Countries with weak economies that knowingly establish offshore zones are necessarily the most permissive.
Oxfam International states, "Some small, poor and vulner-
able economies have found that establishing themselves as
tax havens is an attractive economic option partly because
of the lack of economic alternatives open to them."[7] These
tax havens with no banking or professional credibility usually develop their financial sector to the detriment of the
local population.[8] In a display of incredible financial ava-
rice, the Cayman Islands—"the fifth largest international
financial center and the world hedge fund capital, with $2.3
trillion in funds because of their free and easy acceptance
of international capital," according to *Les Échos*—cannot
manage to handle their current expenses. The financial crisis and a hurricane were enough to bankrupt the
Caymans. The British dependency dared turn to the public

authorities and asked London for support on the order of
$310 million.[9]

The legal residence of corporations has nothing to do
with the physical site of their operations. ICE US Holding
Company L.P. is a Cayman Islands company, but it is at the
same time 50 percent owned by Intercontinental Exchange,
a company headquartered in Atlanta but legally registered
in Delaware, the domestic tax haven of the United States.
ICE US Holding also merged with the Clearing Corporation,
another entity registered in Delaware, created by major international banks Citigroup, Goldman Sachs, J.P. Morgan,
Merrill Lynch, Morgan Stanley, and Bank of America (which
now owns Merrill Lynch), not to mention Deutsche Bank,
UBS, and Credit Suisse. ICE US Holding also has as a business partner, in Delaware again, the near homonym ICE US
Holding Company GP LLC.

What is the business of ICE US Holding? It combines
the advantages of the onshore tax haven of Delaware and
the offshore Cayman Islands tax haven. The clearing system, brought to light by the investigative journalist Lucy
Komisar, deprives the U.S. Treasury of substantial revenue.
"ICE Trust U.S. was created in anticipation of tougher U.S.
laws that will force the trading of derivatives into clearinghouses in which prices are made public and the losses of one
member are shared with others. The Obama Administration
proposed this measure last year, explaining it as a form of
self-insurance designed to reduce the odds of another financial company bailout by U.S. taxpayers," writes Komisar.[10]

The purpose of the measure was in part to combat the
perverse effect of derivatives, financial offerings that bundle
together contracts arising from disparate transactions. Why
was the company set up in the Caymans? Because profits

earned by American companies are not taxed until they are repatriated, for a long time companies maneuvered to have profit-making subsidiaries in tax havens lend money to the parent company in the United States or officially invest in it. This was a way of disguising a profit as something else that would not be taxed. Clearinghouses such as ICE Trust U.S. allowed the owners of capital to refine the repatriation mechanism every time the federal government tried to invalidate the strategy. Rather than investing in or lending directly to its parent company, the foreign subsidiary, by means of accounting devices, advanced sums to a company governed by Cayman Islands law. Komisar explains, "The only reason a Cayman entity was formed was to have a foreign entity in the chain of ownership. . . . This means that banks can keep their profits abroad and untaxed, but still use them to trade on a U.S. exchange, making investments in U.S. credit default swaps while not paying tax on the collateral placed on the exchange."[11]

As reported by the United Nations and repeated by the sociologist Thierry Godefroy and the economist Pierre Lascoumes, several Caribbean states market their sovereignty in this way: "The almost universal abolition of exchange controls and regulatory limits on the circulation of capital, reinforced by the new resources provided by data processing and electronic payment techniques, has created the conditions for the development of financial globalization."[12]

It is precisely that versatility, efficiency, and obscurity made possible by accounting and legal tricks for which European judges and other public officials reproach particularly the Caribbean principalities. Bank secrecy is armor-plated there. Activities of all kinds take place, and the forms in which they are recorded are practically unlimited. Claims of cooperation with international judicial bodies are pure formalities. Marie-Christine Dupuis-Danon, anti-money-laundering advisor to the United Nations Office on Drugs and Crime from 2000 to 2003, points out that "for the money launderer, the search for anonymity is a form of the quest for the Holy Grail. Laws aimed at preventing the laundering of dirty money take on as a priority the identification of users of banking or financial services, but ill-intentioned individuals and organizations still have a good deal of room for maneuver."[13]

For example, in Saint Kitts and Nevis, perversion of the law has reached grotesque proportions. The manager of a trust can also be its trustee and its beneficiary, so the very meaning of the instrument is lost. The beneficiaries in this tiny sovereign state explicitly boast of their opposition to United States law with an arrogance rarely shown to the American empire. As reported by Raymond W. Baker, "Foreign laws, including U.S. laws, do not apply to Nevisian trusts. This means that under Nevisian law, the claim will always have to be re-tried, ab initio, in the Nevisian courts, with Nevisian attorneys, and with Nevisian judges who can generally be expected to uphold the Nevisian trust."[14]

Any employee of local financial services in the Bahamas is subject to imprisonment if he transmits banking information to a third party. This protected world enabled Federal Bank, a shell company originating in Argentina, to take control of Argentine companies and to secure public works contracts with the help of massive corruption.[15]

Panama allows the creation of anonymous accounts. Trusts and holding companies registered there can, without hindrance, manage the operations least likely to be authorized in legitimate states. It is not difficult to find a document praising the expertise of Panamanian banks in the laundering of drug money tied to the traffic from Colombia.[16] Panama also offers flags of convenience, which enable charterers of ships of every category to hire sailors around the world without having to respect any labor code and to conceal the ownership of the vessels.

The Caymans and the Turks and Caicos for their part were home to several of the approximately eight hundred shell companies through which the energy broker Enron concealed its loss-making entities in order to bolster its financial balance sheets.[17]

Bermuda allowed the Swedish-Canadian company Lundin to set up a holding company controlling shares in the Tenke Fungurume Company, which is engaged in extracting copper and cobalt from the mine of the same name in Congo. The company secured mining rights to the site in a one-sided contract conceded by the rebel Laurent-Désiré Kabila at the time he was at war with the dictator Mobutu.[18]

7

DENS OF INDUSTRIAL RELOCATION

In addition to banking and tax havens and secrecy jurisdictions, industrial and production activities developed offshore in free-trade zones and free ports that occupy a central place in the globalization of the economy.

Freed from legal restraints, these development sites were promoted by UNESCO in 1964. Presented as aid to poor countries, zones were established where the new damned of the earth would offer their labor power for less than nothing to relocated Western industries. The Foreign Investment Advisory Service, created by the World Bank in 1985 to "advise developing countries"—in partnership with the heads of large companies—led 117 countries to implement free-trade zones and other financial incentives.[1] Using the pretext of economic development, investors and industrialists greatly profit from these centers of exploitation from another era. The documentary *Let's Make Money* makes the connections between transfers of money facilitated offshore (among pension funds and insurance companies; investment firms in Singapore, London, and other tax havens such as the island of Jersey; real estate speculation seeking only exchange value in Spain) and the subjection of the population of Chennai to the commercial imperatives of the financial elite of the North. In the minds of economic predators, the term "democracy" is summed up by the existence of legal institutions that guarantee gargantuan property rights whose legitimacy is never questioned. The commercial law in force in free-trade zones has supplanted the state itself. The Austrian businessman Mirko Kovats speaks in these terms: "This legal system is very important for me. . . . Here, nobody asks for state aid. Everyone fends for himself." This is why he says he has to "defend" himself "under the pressure of globalization," by planning to impose unpaid overtime "on very badly paid workers who nonetheless have to earn a living," adding, "One cannot afford to be generous."[2] There are no taxes, labor laws, or environmental measures in these "zones," whose number around the world is constantly increasing, going from 79 in 1975 to 2,700 in 2006. They are found in more than a hundred countries, four times more than thirty-five years ago.[3] The example of Jamaica has also produced striking documentaries.[4]

The investigation by the Canadian journalist Naomi Klein of export-processing zones (EPZs) reveals the staggering failure of this "development" strategy:

> Though it has plenty in common with these other tax havens, the export processing zone is really in a class of its own. Less holding tank than sovereign territory, the EPZ is an area where goods don't just pass through but are actually manufactured, an area, furthermore,

where there are no import and export duties, and often no income or property taxes either. . . .

Regardless of where the EPZs are located, the workers' stories have a certain mesmerizing sameness: the workday is long—fourteen hours in Sri Lanka, twelve hours in Indonesia, sixteen in Southern China, twelve in the Philippines. The vast majority of the workers are women, always young, always working for contractors or subcontractors from Korea, Taiwan or Hong Kong. The contractors are usually filling orders for companies based in the U.S., Britain, Japan, Germany or Canada. The management is military-style, the supervisors often abusive, the wages below subsistence and the work low-skill and tedious. As an economic model, today's export processing zones have more in common with fast-food franchises than sustainable developments, so removed are they from the countries that host them. These pockets of pure industry hide behind a cloak of transience: the contracts come and go with little notice; the workers are predominantly migrants, far from home and with little connection to the city or province where zones are located; the work itself is short-term, often not renewed.[5]

Export-processing zones evoke industrial exploitation of another time that sentenced workers to the galleys. Bangladesh, India, Pakistan, and Turkey, for example, bring derelict vessels still full of toxic materials to vast ship graveyards. In this inferno, the workers who dismantle the ships with no equipment and no method risk death at any moment. There is no safety supervision and no real medical care.[6] Every image of the documentary *Shipbreakers* is worth a thousand words.[7]

Export-processing zones would be of no interest if there were no free ports to reduce shipping costs to a minimum. The very fact of the relocation of Western companies can be attributed to these offshore maritime zones. More than 60 percent of freight shipments are carried by ships flying flags of convenience.[8]

By virtue of their sovereignty, the countries that manage the free ports and distribute flags of convenience block the International Maritime Organization (IMO) from oversight. The unrestricted registration they authorize frees shipowners from international maritime labor laws, wage and training requirements, and minimum crew sizes, just as it shelters them from taxation intended to finance public institutions designed precisely to apply safety and environmental standards for the maintenance of ships and the treatment of waste.

It takes no great effort of the imagination to wonder what would happen to the *Exxon Valdez* today if it still existed. It does exist. Renamed the *Dong Fang Ocean*, it now flies the flag of Panama, a well-known free port. From 2005 to 2008, this oil tanker was known as the *Mediterranean*, far from the Alaska waters that had made it notorious. Then it flew the flag of the Marshall Islands, a tax haven and a free port that has maintained administrative ties to the United States, its former tutelary power. Washington used the territory in the late 1940s and early 1950s for large-scale atomic testing. Also a favorite registration site for Japanese ship owners wishing to evade their country's rules, the Marshall Islands have been more widely "developed" and have agreed to register as many as 19,978 oil tankers, according to 2009

UN data, which makes it the fourth-ranking country in the world registering that kind of ship, behind the notorious Panama, Liberia, and Bahamas.[9] Relying on a British source, the tax consultant Édouard Chambost attributes the origin of the Marshall Islands as a free port and that of Liberia to the CIA.[10] And the Marshall Islands is where the renamed *Exxon Valdez* is to be found. Which means that if its hull cracked again and spilled 260,000 barrels of oil, perhaps at the same spot as on March 24, 1989, it would be an arduous task to discover formally the identities of the owner and the user of the ship, as well as to identify the nature of the funds the government could requisition to cover the costs of its intervention.

This is not an apocalyptic hypothesis. BP subcontracted to companies in the Marshall Islands the operation of its *Deepwater Horizon* oil drilling platform in the Gulf of Mexico, the source of an oil spill that may contaminate as much as 40 percent of the Gulf's territorial waters. Because registration of oil drilling platforms follows the model of ship registration, it was to this tax-free, opaque, and highly permissive free port that International Registries, Inc. (IRI) of Virginia brought one of BP's subcontractors to formally register its business. In this case, the company in question was Transocean, a drilling contractor hired by BP to conduct operations in the Gulf of Mexico; it is headquartered in another tax haven, the canton of Zug in Switzerland. International law allows companies to considerably limit their liabilities in the event of an environmental disaster—Transocean's shareholders received $1 billion in dividends only three weeks after the catastrophe. "International maritime law treats drilling platforms as ships, and Transocean's lawyers can ask to limit the company's financial liability in the disaster to the postaccident value of the platform, barely $27 million," writes Khadija Sharife.[11] Sharife, pretending to be acting for a client who wanted to escape regulatory constraints, contacted the registration firm IRI: she was, of course, guaranteed tax exemption for the company, but especially absolute anonymity for its shareholders and managers. "Please note," she was told in an e-mail, "that we are not privy to that information anyway, since all the business organization and conduct of the entity is performed by the entity's lawyers and directors directly."[12]

According to Yobie Benjamin, who blogs on SFGate, the registration of this Swiss drilling contractor in the Marshall Islands makes it impossible for Washington to sue its managers and directors because they are in a secrecy jurisdiction administered by the United States itself.

> By being a Marshall Islands–flagged vessel, the Deepwater Horizon rig is subject to the safety laws and inspection standards of the Marshall Islands. Maritime treaties allow the United States to simply recognize BP's compliance with Marshall Islands' standards as adequate.
>
> Now could the US Justice Department sue the Marshall Islands? I don't think so. That would be like suing ourselves since the US funds the country. Can we sue International Registries Inc (IRI), the company that runs the Marshall Islands' maritime program? Maybe but what are we going to gain by suing IRI, a rinky-dink company that functions as the Marshall Islands' de facto maritime authority?[13]

The lack of regulation of international shipping companies in free ports is matched only by the complacency of legitimate states toward the problem. Rather than denouncing unfair international competition and attacking it formally, France has chosen to bow to the process of dumping by creating a flag of convenience on its own territory, the Registre International Français, intended to keep shipping companies domiciled in France.[14] For more than ten years, the sole shareholder of a shipping company, whose international subsidiary was registered in Barbados, occupied the center of the Canadian political stage, holding in succession between 1993 and 2006 the posts of finance minister and prime minister. His company, Canada Steamship Lines, controlled by a holding company headquartered in Bermuda, with branches in Barbados, Bahamas, and Liberia, was involved in all the sordid aspects of offshore maritime business: tax evasion, the dumping of toxic waste in fishing grounds, transactions with a dictatorial regime, abandonment of a ship in a Turkish maritime graveyard without the knowledge of the country concerned, and even the transport of significant quantities of cocaine.[15]

The European Union, which claims to be concerned by the state of some 4,400 ships in the world fleet, several of which carry dangerous cargo, nonetheless granted substantial political legitimacy to free ports by appointing Joseph Borg as European commissioner for fisheries and maritime affairs in 2004.[16] From 1999 to 2004, Borg had been foreign minister of the Republic of Malta, one of the most controversial free ports in the world. Getting a flag of convenience there is a mere formality. For a nominal fee, almost any ship can be registered, and to manage it one sets up a private company outside the reach of taxation, labor standards, safety constraints, and environmental laws favored by European Union member states. Nearly 10 percent of the world's shipping fleet is registered in Malta.[17]

Taxes are nominal for the island's nonresidents, and this factor has turned out to be decisive. "The Republic of Malta . . . enacted legislation designed to encourage the registration of ships in Malta through tax concessions. Ships have to belong to a qualified Maltese company, a company not subject to any restrictive regulation governing shareholders, officers, or crews," writes André Beauchamp.[18] A clause on double taxation permits shareholders who register their assets on the island to deduct taxes so that they pay only 4.17 percent. The offer is so attractive that even state-owned ships of Poland are registered there.

Malta also specializes in networks of notoriously Mafia-linked activities, such as gambling and gaming, while at the same time becoming one of the most important online European financial centers and the world center for electronic payments. Also, anyone with assets on the order of €5 million can establish a bank there. Although he is an apologist for tax havens, in the latest edition of his guide, Grégoire Duhamel says of Malta that it is a site where "suspect money" is concentrated, and for that reason he gives it an average grade of only 11.5 out of 20.[19]

This mixture of mafiosi and international shippers is not without consequences: between 1996 and 1998, 443 ships registered in the Republic of Malta failed to meet international safety standards, and the average age of the Maltese fleet—about twenty years—was among the highest in the world. The Bretons, who saw the *Erika* dump 30,000 tons of fuel oil along their coast in 1999, were not very happy. The ship's owner, Tevere Shipping, was registered in Malta, and another Maltese company, Camillieri, was involved in running the ship. Because banking secrecy is in force in Malta, the island allows numbered accounts; such an opaque system prevents practically any investigation into the responsibilities for a disaster such as that of the *Erika*.

In another case, the ship *Kristal* broke in two off the port of La Corogne in Spain. Witnesses were terrified. Luckily, it was transporting only molasses. It, too, was registered in Malta.[20]

The fate of *Erika* and *Kristal* is not an exception in offshore annals. As a general matter, free ports guarantee impunity, encourage carelessness, and authorize environmental negligence. In Ivory Coast in 2006, the captain of the *Probo Koala* is reported to have knowingly dumped toxic waste off the coast, producing an environmental catastrophe. Gilles Labarthe writes:

> More than 528 cubic meters primarily of hydrogen sulfide (H_2S), sodium hydroxide (NaOH) and mercaptan—highly toxic substances that can cause death—were dumped at seven sites identified so far around the capital, beginning on August 19, 2006. A Russian ship flying a Panamanian flag, the *Probo Koala*, that had arrived the day before, discharged its "slops"—officially waste water containing a small quantity of oil—for more than 30 hours as though it were routine. In reality its chemical disposal was much deadlier. How did the *Probo Koala* receive authorization to dock in Ivory Coast, when it had been turned away from Guinea, Liberia, Sierra Leone, and Nigeria in succession because of its highly toxic cargo? As usual for maritime shipments of petroleum and chemical products, the *Probo Koala* has clouded the issue, flying a flag of convenience from a Caribbean tax haven. It also has a multiplicity of intermediaries.[21]

Eight to fifteen people died as a result of what most people would see as an economic crime. Several tens of thousands of people had to take refuge in the interior of the country or suffered other harm.

In any event, offshore sirens are pursued by legitimate states themselves. Jean de Maillard writes, "Take France. For arms sales and large oil or aircraft contracts, the government uses tax havens. France's public debt is dependent on financial markets with its speculative funds swollen with money of all kinds."[22] And the so-called rich countries exhibit such a strong tendency to follow the logic of poor countries to attract at any cost sacrosanct finance capital that they have adopted the same methods. This is the case with Halifax, Canada, a financial center linked to Bermuda since 2006.[23] The same phenomenon can also be clearly seen in Belgium.[24]

It has therefore become impossible, where banking secrecy holds sway, to separate public interests, so-called legitimate economic interests, and criminal interests. A trading company can, for example, be financed by illegal trafficking and along the way adopt mechanisms to launder capital derived from those operations, making it impossible to have a clear idea of what has happened. This is because the vast majority of trading companies have offshore subsidiaries where a substantial proportion of their transactions is conducted. One of China's largest trading partners is the British Virgin Islands. Because funds transfers take place with no oversight, there is nothing enabling us to distinguish today between the prodigious amount of global criminal activity and legitimate commercial transactions. As a consequence, profits from the drug trade can finance the opening of a chain of clothing stores. The criminal economy should now be seen as a vast network, some parts of which necessarily operate in law-governed areas and others in completely opaque zones in ways impossible to disentangle.

In that sense, tax havens are less geographical sites than an accounting device to register specific assets that call for discretion. This is why de Maillard writes: "The considerable growth of banking havens and offshore companies came in parallel to the increase in bogus transactions dictated solely by the need to conceal dirty money. Why were these criminal havens allowed to proliferate? Because covert finance has all the appearances of legitimate finance. It shares the same circuits and fulfills the same requirements of solvency and credit."[25]

This contradicts the claims of economic liberalism that all rational agents in a market share the same information that they are at liberty to interpret and on the basis of which they can make enlightened decisions. On the contrary, to be a serious economist or investor today requires including the blind spot of criminal finance in the interstices of official data. That is where industry has taken off.

8

PLUNDER REGISTERED OFFSHORE

It might be thought that July 15, 2010, marked a step forward in the fight to control controversial branches of industry. On that date, the Senate gave final approval to the Dodd-Frank Wall Street Reform and Consumer Protection Act.

The Dodd-Frank Act required that mining and oil companies registered with the SEC make public their expenditures to both foreign and U.S. governments to gain access to resources. The international organization Publish What You Pay was pleased to see a measure it had been promoting for a long time take concrete form as a law. A bill along the same lines, the Extractive Industries Transparency Disclosure Act, had long been under consideration by the Congress.

The Congo Conflict Minerals Act (introduced in the Senate in April 2009, but not adopted) contains a provision aimed at cutting off support to armed groups profiting from trade in metals incorporated in high-technology products. The law would require U.S. companies doing business in the Democratic Republic of Congo (DRC) to declare annually to the SEC where they obtain tin oxide, coltan, wolframite, and gold. Although this measure is directed against corrupt entities in the South (armed groups) rather than the corrupters from the North (mining companies), prominent NGOs nevertheless believe it would be a step forward; they include Global Witness in England, and in the United States, Catholic Relief Services and John Prendergast of the Enough Project, who said: "The world moved a step closer to ensuring that the supply chains for our laptops and cell phones do not finance violence in eastern Congo."[1]

Several mining and oil multinationals are, of course, incorporated in the United States. But, even if it secures passage, will this measure be effective, considering that the vast majority of such companies are headquartered in the discreet neighbor to the north, Canada, a regulatory paradise adapted to their requirements?

Imagine the surprise of Christophe Lutundula, member of the Congolese parliament and president of a 2003 commission charged with investigating the validity of contracts signed by his countrymen, when he realized that even if one knew the identity of the companies that held mining concessions obtained in suspicious wartime circumstances, the concessions had been awarded on the basis of agreements signed with bodies whose assets were located in tax havens. How could he review a contract signed under unacceptable conditions when the local participants were desperately seeking finance and weapons, the company involved was the Lundin mining empire (controlled by the Lundin Holding Company of Bermuda), and the Vancouver-based Tenke Fungurume Mining (in which Lundin held an interest) was represented in Congo by former prime minister Jean Chrétien of Canada? With whom could he discuss the controversial agreement of the government with the Kinross-Forrest joint venture when the latter entity was registered in the British Virgin Islands? How could he question the Montreal company Emaxon, controlled by the Israeli diamond magnate Dan Gertler through other Caribbean tax havens that could not be identified with certainty? How could he rescind an agreement with Vin Mart Canada, whose owners and place of registration were completely unknown? How could he call to account Panorama Resources of Vancouver when even the UN could not identify its owners? In his report, Lutundula questioned the purposes of these registrations in secrecy jurisdictions.[2]

This architecture of world finance is instructive. It evidences a triangular relationship between imperialist nations supposedly governed by law, countries of the South subject to trade and economic forces beyond their control, and tax havens. Offshore interests dominate this triangle and are not controlled by any center.

In the imperialist nations, offshore interests increase the value of their assets in the stock markets where they are listed and attract the capital they may need for development projects in the countries of the South. The case of Canada in the area of mining is particularly eloquent. Seventy percent of the world's mining companies are registered in Canada. Not only do they enjoy choice infrastructures for setting up and changing location, formally registering their business, employing a healthy, educated (and if necessary alienated) workforce, and airtight security for their assets, but they also receive massive subsidies from the authorities and find significant sources of finance in various public funds. What is more, Canada's federal and provincial institutions have done everything possible to foster private institutional investment in the mining sector (which had a stock volume of $450 billion Canadian in 2008) while providing legal cover against any judicial action for the abuses widely attributed to the industry outside Canadian borders. Hence, it is Canadian citizens, with their taxes and various contributions and savings, who substantially support the mining projects in the South. Toronto has become the piggy bank for the mining industry, a pipeline of money that supports most mining projects around the world, even the most polluting, unjust, or insane. "Generally speaking, in the mining industry, risk capital comes from Canada," the engineer René Nollevaux confirmed as though it were obvious when he was interviewed by Thierry Michel for his film *Katanga Business*.[3] Nollevaux was preparing to receive Canadian and British investors interested in the Katanga mine, managed by the Canadian company Katanga Mining, which in turn was controlled by the Belgian George Forrest. The documentary then describes extensively the expropriation of small-scale miners, police repression of strikers, and the smuggling common at the province's borders. It is estimated that the government loses $20 million in customs duties in a single day.

The tale is well known. Respectable mining companies from the North, created on occasion by arms dealers or hustlers, indulge in the South in everything required by the laws of competition to gain access to mineral deposits. One-sided contracts, corruption, pillage, violent or even deadly expropriation, and collusion with corrupt national armies or warlords are not uncommon—and all require in turn the participation of secrecy jurisdictions, not to mention the environmental controversy provoked by most projects in the affected communities. In these circumstances, one wonders what public body can still politically oversee, for example, a company such as Heritage Oil of Calgary, founded by the mercenary Tony Buckingham, a former partner of Executive Outcomes, notorious for its bloody activities in Angola and Sierra Leone. Following opaque negotiations, the company now holds an oil concession on the border between the DRC and Uganda. Canada refuses to supervise rigorously the world mining industry, the majority of which is registered in the country, except to provide it with financial support. For civil society, therefore, it seems very difficult, if not impossible, to sue Canadian companies for misdeeds committed outside the country's borders. Heritage Oil, like many other companies, is covered by the judicial haven that Canada has turned out to be in the mining sector, while at the same time developing other services offshore, for example, its finance and management center in Switzerland.

The South is thus turned over to lawless exploitation. As John Perkins, a repentant "economic hit man," has described the system, the idea is to put the nations of the South into debt for overvalued and unsuitable projects that profit only private bodies and thereby gain access indefinitely, because of the relation of economic dependence, to their essential natural resources. No public body is a match for foreign investors.[4] Even before it takes any action in one industry or another, the extraordinary power of the dominant class, which David Rothkopf calls the "superclass," is explained primarily by the fact that it has exclusive access to resources of all kinds: "For the members of the superclass, there is a commodity more precious than gold, silver, gems, or oil. It is access."[5] Management practices known as "good governance," when they are applied, at most allow states in the South to transform themselves into brokers offering their wealth on ever more favorable conditions. The chronic debt spiral into which the financial players of the North have plunged them

subjects them to an increasingly pathetic search for foreign
capital, at the risk of selling off almost everything. The treasuries of African states are bled dry while Western investors,
financed by pension funds and other institutional investors,
try to get share prices of Toronto mining start-ups to soar or
to maintain their already established empires in the sector.
One can guess that corruption, managed from numbered
accounts, keeps the machinery well oiled. This kind of manipulation prevails in mining as well as the energy and food
processing sectors.

Not only do the populations of the South suffer the political and environmental consequences of the industrial exploitation of their resources, but they also receive virtually
no proceeds from these activities. Systematic tax evasion and
tax avoidance is child's play. In the 1990s and beyond, under the pressure of international institutions, mining codes
outrageously advantageous to the mining industry appeared
in the countries of the South; the codes were strangely similar to those Canada had inherited from its colonial economy. They provide for tax holidays or very low tax rates for
companies, not to mention the tax evasion that is rife, as
noted in increasingly urgent reports on the question, notably in Tanzania.[6] In 2009, Oxfam International cautiously
estimated the annual loss of earnings of developing countries because of offshore activities at $124 billion, enough to
finance many public services in the areas of education and
health.[7]

Populations in the North nonetheless have some reasons to feel solidarity with those in the South, because although the companies they finance by their taxes and their
forced contributions to the stock market bring them profit,
the same companies have a thousand ways to avoid pay-

ing taxes in those countries by recording their dividends offshore.

Illicit capital flight from Africa is estimated at between $854 billion and $1.8 trillion from 1970 to 2008, at least $29 billion annually, by the United States organization Global Financial Integrity.[8]

The financial circuits of the mining industry follow a triangular itinerary, from Canada, which supplies the liquid assets, to the mining companies established in the South to develop the mines, to the tax havens where the profits are deposited.

9

DELAWARE, USA:
THE DOMESTIC HAVEN

The tone was grandiloquent and the action was intended to be serious. On May 4, 2009, President Obama rose up against tax havens. His solemn speech stressed the importance of the coming confrontation to such a degree that it was surprising to realize how weak the adversary was: a few second-rate countries in what people liked to call "old Europe," and some Caribbean islands with unfamiliar names. The esthetic tinged with dark humor of offshore tax consultants had done its work. A president staring down a dispersed, eccentric, and therefore insignificant enemy looked slightly ridiculous. How was it possible to imagine the United States beating its chest in defiance of states such as the Swiss Confederation and the Cayman Islands?

If the global order of sovereign states conformed to its theoretical representation, it goes without saying that the political authority of the United States would make short work of these microstates. But they sometimes openly laugh at the

United States in a way that the head of an Islamist state, even one with nuclear weapons, would not dare to.

And the president presented himself as being on the defensive. This opponent fell outside the convenient rhetoric of a clash of civilizations attributing all fault to a radically foreign adversary who was, of course, "anti-American." It soon became apparent that a domestic war was at issue. From these small states came harbingers of internal guerilla warfare. This explains why Obama soothed the nation's sensitivities even before attacking the enemy. "Let's begin with a simple premise: nobody likes paying taxes, particularly in times of economic stress. But most Americans meet their responsibilities because they understand that it's an obligation of citizenship, necessary to pay the costs of our common defense and our mutual well-being." Paying taxes to foster the emergence of shared benefits that one could never enjoy if one relied only on one's own resources turns out to be even more controversial in the United States than the fact of discarding such benefits by evading taxes to the detriment of the entire community. This is why Obama felt compelled before anything else to set out an ideological premise and immediately associate taxes with the specific concerns of national defense. The portion of the U.S. budget devoted to the armed forces is indeed disproportionate, but the time had not yet come for the essential debate on whether the national effort to fill the public coffers would be better rewarded by the development of public services that would really benefit the majority: a truly universal health care system, social programs making it possible for the American dream to have a semblance of meaning for the millions of Americans now born in third-world poverty, and educational institutions providing students with instruction that would make them responsible citizens.

The president focused instead on companies that must "remain the most competitive in the world" and on the creation of jobs for the underprivileged that the closing of tax loopholes would bring about. The social measures he alluded to involved tax breaks for training programs or home purchases. He did not speak of the state's interest in increasing its revenues in order to carry out public policies to benefit the population as a whole.

Because it is not a good idea to state the whole truth, the inquiry as to the hemorrhagic proportions of capital flight to offshore centers was put off. It was important not to point out that half the world's financial transactions pass through dummy jurisdictions, or that tax evasion holds no mysteries for any multinational, or that $250 billion is laundered annually in the United States, according to official data that are probably underestimates.[1] The phenomenon was reduced to a small number of offenders, marginal and anonymous. And promises were made of "tax breaks to companies that create jobs here in America," tax benefits for the accumulation of private wealth derived from the labor of a mass of atomized wage-earners.

This speech by Obama nonetheless deserves respect: he probably went as far as a president of the United States could go, one who was electorally indebted to the financial elite. He continued:

> And many are aided and abetted by a broken tax system, written by well-connected lobbyists on behalf of well-heeled interests and individuals. It's a tax code full of corporate loopholes that makes it perfectly legal for companies to avoid paying their fair share. It's a tax code that makes it all too easy for a number—a small

number of individuals and companies to abuse overseas tax havens to avoid paying any taxes at all. And
it's a tax code that says you should pay lower taxes if
you create a job in Bangalore, India, than if you create
one in Buffalo, New York.

The enemy is within, and the president recognized
it. But how many rhetorical contortions did he have to go
through to depict a tax system it is "all too easy" to get
around, while at the same time only "a small number of individuals and companies" abuse it? And yet, inexorably, those
companies turn up in the president's speech as the "subsidiaries of some of our largest companies," whose personnel
were trained in business schools and by conventional economic wisdom to obsessively pursue cost savings, a category
including taxes.

The fight against tax havens not only revealed a domestic flaw but was diverted onto the domestic scene. The
Obama administration might very well stigmatize the
Cayman Islands as "the largest tax scam," able to house
twelve thousand companies in a single building; it was as
though, even in presidential speeches, the islands were a mirage of the offshore esthetic of the image of paradise, and
their reality was out of reach. The fight had to be domestic to
arm Americans against the temptations of that mirage. The
federal authorities tried to get Americans themselves to declare their offshore income. The government announced that
it was hiring eight hundred IRS agents to tighten controls.
Following the speech, Congress ratified the Unemployment
Compensation Extension Act of 2010 (HR 4213). The law
joined the extension of minor tax deductions and credits tied
to economic recovery with the closing of loopholes, particu-

larly with respect to tax havens. It had the virtue of ending some aberrations in the U.S. tax code, such as the wrongful deduction of tax expenditures in foreign jurisdictions although no similar tax had really been paid in the United States; the transformation, advantageous in terms of taxation, of individual income into capital gains; and the tricks used by several corporations to evade Social Security and Medicare taxes.[2] In its wake and in the same spirit, the Close Big Oil Tax Loopholes Act (S. 3405) was adopted on May 24, 2010. Another bill, the Incorporation Transparency and Law Enforcement Assistance Act, aimed at requiring the disclosure of the owners of any corporation or limited liability company established on U.S. territory, was introduced in the Senate on March 11, 2009. With these changes, the White House expected it would keep more than $200 billion in the United States between 2010 and 2019.

But Barack Obama never put direct pressure on tax havens themselves, except for some rhetorical attacks before he took office.[3] Tax havens continue undisturbed in making unavailable the expected information. The "set of proposals to crack down on illegal overseas tax evasion" was thus aimed not at a rival jurisdiction created out of whole cloth by financial and legal sorcerer's apprentices to harm established states but at "evasion itself." The United States has historically been more vindictive.

Even Democratic lawmakers greeted Obama's timid tax reform initiatives coldly. Joseph Crowley, a member of the tax-writing House Ways and Means Committee, declared his opposition to any change in the tax code that would "harm" Citigroup, Inc., on the grounds that it was the largest employer in his congressional district.[4] This reaction from Ryan J. Donmoyer of Bloomberg was in the order of things: "Many corporate lobbyists expected Obama would repeal the entire deferral system altogether. That fear whipped up enough hysteria to motivate more than 200 large companies—including IBM, Coca-Cola, Caterpillar, Procter & Gamble, Cisco, GE, DuPont, and Eli Lilly—to send congressional leaders a letter objecting to Obama's proposal weeks before it was even released."[5] Charlie Cray, who made this observation, added that several multinationals were still saving millions of dollars in taxes by transferring their assets offshore. The Obama administration's timid measures enabled it to avoid facing the basic problem that "U.S. multinational corporations enjoy an effective tax rate of just 2.4 percent on billions of dollars in foreign active earnings," says Cray.[6]

DELAWARE: THE WHITE HOUSE'S PROTÉGÉ

According to President Obama, the issue was not simply tax evasion, but the convoluted phenomenon of "illegal overseas tax evasion." Was the president indicating that tax evasion was in fact illegal? Did he intend to say that he wanted to end the illegal variety, meaning that tax evasion might turn out to be legal in some circumstances, such as when the government he presided over made it legal? Perhaps that meant when it was not overseas, but in Delaware, an offshore state within the United States, which was represented in the Senate for thirty-six years by Vice President Joseph Biden.

Primarily because of "modern and flexible corporate laws" and "a business-friendly State Government," in this small state (population less than 800,000) "more than 850,000 business entities have their legal home . . . including more than 50% of all U. S. publicly-traded companies and 63% of the Fortune 500," according to the state government itself.[7]

Delaware behaves like any other tax haven. It guarantees banking secrecy and minimal or zero tax rates to foreign investors. These investors can therefore take advantage of U.S. jurisdiction without paying taxes, and in addition avoid having the public or the authorities know the nature of their business activities and the state of their accounts, as long as they are not publicly traded. A specialty of the U.S. tax system is that personal taxation is levied depending on U.S. citizenship. Recalling that point, and relying on the offshore investment consulting firm OCRA International, the Tax Justice Network has evaluated the serious consequences of that premise. Because Delaware allows foreign individuals to avoid the constraints related to U.S. citizenship, they manage with relative ease to evade the federal government's taxation requirements. The U.S. authorities have no accounting or banking information on these individuals in Delaware, which leaves the authorities unequipped to cooperate with foreign police or judicial services requesting information about them.

This state of affairs has a direct effect on the U.S. economy because many bodies registered in the United States go through foreign subsidiaries to enjoy these benefits exactly as though the U.S.-registered companies were foreign. The Tax Justice Network explains:

> A financial institution outside of the United States, such as a foreign (non-US) financial institution or a foreign (non-US) branch of a US financial institution, can become a qualified intermediary (QI) by submitting an application to the US Internal Revenue Service and agreeing to comply with the QI requirements in the US Internal Revenue Code. The advantage of QI

> status is that foreign persons (individuals and compa-
> nies) can invest in the United states through the QI,
> with the QI complying with Know Your Customer re-
> quirements (KYC). The QI maintains outside of the
> United States information about the identity of each
> foreign investor and the KYC information about each
> foreign investor, but the QI invests in the United States
> in the name of the QI rather than in the name of the
> foreign investor.[8]

The volumes involved are considerable. The QI program has drawn investments to the United States on the order of $600–$650 billion, according to 2007 data from the Government Accountability Office (GAO). These foreign, and possibly domestic, funds elude taxation and legal oversight by the public authorities. For these reasons, the Tax Justice Network has placed the United States in the front rank of its world index of opacity of tax havens.

Creating a limited liability company in Delaware not only enabled U.S. companies to escape their community responsibilities but also allowed a multitude of foreign entities, small and large, to cause the same harm to their own communities by registering in Delaware for accounting purposes even though they conduct no business there. According to an assessment by *The Economist* of a study by the Australian analyst Jason Sharman, "For foreigners, America is a particularly attractive place to stash cash, because it does not tax the interest income they earn. Thus with both anonymity and no taxation, America offers them all the elements of a tax haven."[9] One is reminded of a catalogue out of Borges: Delaware is very advantageous for professionals working in sectors as varied as intellectual and artistic production, the Internet, freelance work, multimedia, work at home, "and all those that generate income in whole or in part from abroad," according to the online consulting firm Axefirm.[10] You can set up a company in less than a day in this permissive state, with the bonus of "a business address service," as well as "a bank for your company." What is the reason for this detour? "No corporate taxes, anonymity of directors and shareholders, speed of incorporation, very low creation and maintenance costs," not to mention access from everywhere to the bank account you open there.[11] This opening of Delaware to all the tricksters of accounting is directed as far as China; Mandarin is the only language other than English in which the State of Delaware itself boasts of its favorable tax climate on its official website.[12]

Many international tax experts, including the French idolator of offshore finance Grégoire Duhamel, are unstinting in their praise of Delaware: "All meetings can be held outside Delaware. A single person can be simultaneously director, president, secretary, and treasurer, as well as sole shareholder, without residing in the Unites States."[13]

The lawyer Gideon Rothschild encourages his clients to divide their assets between Saint Kitts and Nevis, the Cook Islands, and Delaware trusts. "It makes it harder for a creditor if they have to fight the battle on different fronts," he explains.[14]

It is not surprising that permissive states such as Delaware, Nevada, Oregon, and Montana have legalized sports betting, for example. They have tried to neutralize any measure adopted elsewhere aimed at regulating public life. Public institutions are aimed at taking political subjects out of the state of nature, but jurisdictions of convenience have created a paradoxical legal system that returns us to the state of nature.

It was easy for the representatives of jurisdictions of convenience explicitly targeted by the American administration in the May 4, 2009, speech or at international summits to hold a mirror up to the administration. "The G20 has no credibility as an undertaking if Delaware, Wyoming or Nevada or far-flung islands from the United States are not on the blacklist," said Prime Minister Jean-Claude Juncker of Luxembourg in April 2009, and he knows something about the issue.[15] According to a Swiss report, a single building on North Orange Street in Wilmington was the theoretical residence of 200,000 companies.[16] "Many of them are empty shells," added the Cayman Islands daily *Caymanian Compass*, proudly reprinting an article that appeared first in the *New York Times*.[17] *The Guardian*, for its part, revealed the names of some prestigious beneficiaries of these deceptive practices: Ford, American Airlines, General Motors, Coca-Cola, and Kentucky Fried Chicken.[18] And the *Village Voice* turned its spotlight on the businessman mayor of New York, Michael Bloomberg: "Most of the Bloomberg entities, including Bloomberg Cayman Islands LLC, are registered at 2711 Centreville Road, Suite 400, in Wilmington, Delaware, an address that also houses thousands of other businesses, including Boeing, UBS, and Lexis Nexis."[19]

In the same season, a propagator of the good news about offshore investing published in a Swiss weekly a story about this exchange of favors: the first choice of most large Swiss companies for registration was Delaware to avoid paying Swiss taxes. Yves Steiner writes in *L'Hebdo*, "For the companies listed on the Swiss Market Index (SMI) of the Zurich Stock Market alone, nearly one third of their foreign entities are located in these tax havens of peace. In the Caribbean mini-islands or Luxembourg, but primarily in the United

States, mainly Delaware, and the United Kingdom."[20] A deputy from the depraved country of Russia added his two cents: Vladislav Reznik, chairman of a parliamentary committee on financial markets, expressed his surprise at the fact that the greatest concentration of offshore companies in the world was in Delaware, a statement that the international press was quick to report.

Australia's tax office wrote to the U.S. Senate Committee on Homeland Security and Governmental Affairs that "in our opinion, entities established in some states of the USA, for example some US incorporated companies, have some of these same attributes as entities established in secrecy havens."[21] (Australia is now developing its own jurisdictions of convenience.)[22]

In her book *Le secret bancaire est mort, vive l'évasion fiscale*, the assistant editor of the Swiss financial magazine *Bilan*, Myret Zaki, considers that through the "anti-tax haven" charges by the G20 and the OECD against European jurisdictions of convenience, the United States and the United Kingdom are attempting to establish the hegemony of tax havens under Anglo-Saxon control.[23] By encrypting internally an ever more sophisticated jurisdiction of convenience, Americans and Britons have exempted capital in all its forms from taxation within their jurisdictions, thereby often making offshore banking secrecy obsolete.

The entire system of trusts is particularly at issue. Thanks to this system, holders of assets present themselves to legal and tax authorities as unrelated to their own wealth, because they have entrusted it to the Anglo-Saxon legal entity the trust. This legal fiction permits anonymity; the trustees may themselves be ignorant of the person for whose benefit they are administrating the property entrusted to them.

The most extravagant tax havens—those in the Caribbean, for example—sometimes allow the beneficiary to be the trustee at the same time, which simply violates the meaning of words. The fact remains that in its standard form, this invention, the trust, damages the spirit of the modern state in its supposed ability to manage public life with full knowledge and impose on it at least some degree of regulation. The state is deprived of the conditions for accomplishing this task by the establishment of the trust system for managing private wealth.[24]

Stéphane Benoît-Godet of Abroad-Consulting.com is in complete agreement: "By targeting Swiss bank secrecy, the 'war against tax evasion' means to be highly moral. But the reality is entirely different: this is a purely commercial war against Switzerland. The war aims at the recovery of market share in funds management from Switzerland by the Anglo-Saxon financial industry."[25] He evaluates at $5 trillion the undeclared funds deposited in Delaware, and estimates that U.S. citizens conceal $1.6 trillion from their tax authorities. The charge against Switzerland, a country that claims to handle only 1.25 percent of that American evasion, seems to arise from unspoken motives.

It is a mystery to few that Obama's attack on European tax havens, particularly Switzerland, was aimed more at consolidating centers managed by Anglo-Saxon interests than at undermining the offshore phenomenon as such.

This amounted to an announcement of "the end of tax havens," but it was an end of the most depressing kind: offshore dumping had sufficiently done its work within traditional states that the powerful could do without small tax havens with bad reputations.

In response, expert wordsmiths in tax matters presented a highly nuanced defense of the democratic virtues of Delaware in order to distinguish it from gangster offshore jurisdictions such as Bermuda and the Seychelles, former colonial subjects always easy to blame. "Delaware, a Legal Rather than a Tax Haven" was the headline in the French financial daily *Les Échos*, full of philosophical subtlety that day. "Wrongly vilified as an American tax haven, Delaware is primarily a haven for corporate lawyers, who find there one of the most modern and effective corporation statutes in the country," writes Virginie Robert.[26] For these licensed rhetoricians acting as business reporters, the fact that American states, not only the emblematic Delaware but also Nevada, Wyoming, and South Dakota, "impose no corporate or personal income tax" makes them at most states "often mentioned as potential tax havens."[27] Some disputed the offshore status of Delaware by insisting on the legality of the operations the state itself authorizes. An example is provided by Nicholas Mirkay, professor at Widener University School of Law: "I never thought of Delaware as a tax haven in the way that people think of the Caymans or other places where you're able to shelter lots of assets from income tax."[28] Who needs to talk about hiding anything when the jurisdiction in question has so perverted itself that it makes problematic acts legitimate?

Nevada defends itself vigorously from being placed in the category of states of convenience. Nevada is not a tax haven; it merely offers "a very attractive tax climate that makes it a good place to do business," in the language of government spokesman Daniel Burns.[29] According to Secretary of State Ross Miller, Nevada "should never be confused with a lack of transparency in some international banking jurisdictions"; however, the IRS had launched an investigation of many companies registered in the state that "do not file tax returns," notes John G. Edwards in the *Las Vegas Review-Journal*.[30] The devil is in the details.

The example of the United States makes it clear that acting "offshore" means operating not literally off the coast of institutionally structured countries but beyond the control of any public institution, in jurisdictions whose law reduces subjects legally to the state of nature, a state of barbarity inevitably damaging to the greatest number, a state from which constitutional projects have always attempted to free us.

THE ORIGIN OF TAX HAVENS:
AN AMERICAN SUCCESS STORY

As a domestic American jurisdiction of convenience, Delaware significantly contributed to the rise of the corporation as a body capable of competing with the sovereign prerogatives of political entities, including nation-states. Before becoming a well-known tax haven, Delaware, like New Jersey, established itself as a regulatory haven. It was a period when the judiciary, corrupted by financial power—to the extent that, in Aristotle's sense, the modification went so far as to change one thing into another—removed from governments their claim to exercise authority over private companies. Before 1886, private companies tended to be creatures of government, not the opposite. Dedicated to the defense of the common good, states, in the best instances, authorized the incorporation of companies only within strict limits: a corporation existed for a limited period and had a precise mandate (development of a mine, construction of a dam, extension of a railway line), and the charter issued in its name was specifically tailored to its size and mandate. Authorizations for incorporation were also revocable by states as soon as they had doubts about the validity of the corporations' business. Most important, shareholders were personally liable for losses incurred by the enterprise they co-financed and that earned them income. The aim was to establish a distinction with the colonial countermodel, from which the Americans had just gained their freedom, of monopolistic companies supported by the Crown to the detriment of cooperatives and small enterprises. Richard L. Grossman and Frank I. Adams write, "Kings appointed governors and judges; dispatched soldiers; dictated taxes, investments, production, labor, and market. The royal charter creating Maryland, for example, required that the colony's exports be shipped to or through England."[31] Corporations had to be prevented from becoming rulers in turn. The United States in the nineteenth century was permeated by debates between supporters of institutions watching out for the common good and advocates of financial sovereignty reigning over the huge quantities of property that capital had seized. The disagreement grew in magnitude as control over labor, hence of the economy, then of the press and of elections entered into contention, and concluded with control over deliberative bodies and the laws passed in the name of the general public.

Politically, the shock of the Civil War sounded the death knell for aspirations for rigorous control over common resources. Decimated by serious human and material losses, governments found themselves subject to blackmail by holders of capital. Grossman and Adams write, "Government spending during the Civil War brought these corporations fantastic wealth. Corporate managers developed the techniques and the ability to organize production on an ever grander scale. Many corporations used their wealth to take advantage of war and Reconstruction years to get the tariff, banking, railroad, labor, and public lands legislation they wanted."[32]

During the same period, high finance took advantage of favorable judicial opinions to impose its will. In the course of the nineteenth century, there was a movement away from incisive decisions by state courts essentially directed toward defense of the "public good" and thereby challenging any "privilege" corporations might seek to secure. In a decision that seems contorted to common sense, the ghost of colonization reappeared in 1819, but this time in favor of private interests. The Supreme Court held that a state did not have the right to intervene in the management of an institution, in this case Dartmouth College, on the grounds that it was founded by George III in the colonial period (*Dartmouth College v. Woodward*). Indeed, when George III approved the charter in 1769, the document did not provide for its possible amendment by a public body that did not yet exist.

The fatal blow had to be struck sooner or later. In 1886, in the context of a tax case, by means of a logically monstrous fiction to which the judiciary was able to give real historical moment, the Supreme Court granted corporations rights until then allotted to persons. For this purpose the court relied on the Fourteenth Amendment, although it had been passed by Congress in order to define citizenship in a way that would ensure that newly freed blacks would be recognized and protected by the government.

Slowly but surely, judges appointed by governments decreasingly in control of affairs twisted the meaning of the Constitution and displayed contempt for its spirit in order to arm capital with all the protections of constitutional law.

It was an era of paradoxical perversions. In a perversion of politics, the government undermined itself by officially endorsing the plastic concept of due process of law as a device to protect constitutional subjects against the government itself, rather than forcing itself as a government to neutralize any citizen causing harm to others.

There was a perversion of law by itself, which culminated when judges ended up protecting corporations against any harm they might suffer from governments or citizens, such as strikers, rather than considering the wrong corporations caused by their increasing activity. Over time, courts declared unconstitutional, because harmful to the interests of corporations, a good many public measures aimed at protecting workers and employees in the private sector. Manipulated behind the scenes by financial interests, this law and the institutions that enforced it legitimated the interpretation that workers are a production fuel at the disposal of corporations that need them. This perversion of law was initiated by the institution that was its target. It was a twofold perversion suffered by law because of decisions made by legal bodies themselves in the name of law itself.

The political principles that presided over the American Revolution and founded the constitutional project of the liberated states, which led to a belated recognition of the rights of African Americans, were distorted by the courts to foster the colonization of the territory by sovereign entities that were no longer monarchical but financial. No public debate and no particular legislation on corporations took place to bring about this recognition as citizens of fictitious entities that were in no way the same as individuals. This recognition as "persons" of immortal entities infinitely representable everywhere came about in the name of egalitarian principles. It is still the basis of an ideology, wrongly called individualist, that still feeds on this sophism.

The advantages offered by Delaware in these circumstances were ready to be picked like ripe fruit. This state allows private interests to go beyond the stage of blackmailing the government so that they have obtained absolutely tailor-made legislation. Armed with their new constitutional prerogatives and Delaware's name as a regulatory haven, corporations there were able to free themselves of any public control, to last over time, to release their shareholders from any liability for what they did, to merge with each other, and to endlessly diversify their investments in the most heterogeneous sectors (food processing at the same time as financial services and heavy engineering).

Robert Hare, a psychologist consulted by the FBI on the profile of the psychopath, describes the corporation—considered as a person—as resembling the psychopaths he has treated in his practice. Laying claim to a potentially eternal life span and the gift of ubiquity whenever it delegates someone to represent it anywhere in the world, the corporation, in Hare's eyes, displays cynical indifference to the feelings of others, instability in outside relations, contempt for issues of public safety, abuse and manipulation of whoever provides a means to achieve an end, lack of capacity for remorse, shame, or guilt, and inability to behave socially according to the elementary rules of conduct or of the law. Law professor Joel Bakan used Hare's testimony in a work on the form the corporation has taken on in Delaware.[33]

What is observable today was described by the philosopher Georg Simmel in 1896: "Thus, people of otherwise great personal integrity have taken part in establishing the most opaque companies, and many people are inclined to behave with much less moral conscience and in a more dubious fashion in matters dealing purely with money than when there is a question of doing something ethically dubious in other relations."[34] If the corporation can without difficulty be described theoretically as a psychopathic "person," its directors appear to be schizophrenics insofar as the autonomous status of the corporation as a legal entity serves them as a psychic screen and enables them to give free rein, in the name of that fictitious subjectivity they embody for a few hours each day, to an extraordinary release of impulses that they themselves would consider asocial once they recovered their own personality in civil life. Moreover they are assiduous churchgoers and openly proclaim their religious observance, and are eager to donate huge sums to charity or public institutions, when they are not busy attending ceremonies for the distribution of awards handed out by a group never shy about self-congratulation. Samir Gibara observes not only how "powerless" governments have become in the face of corporations but also that as CEO of Goodyear, he was not able to act according to his conscience in the exercise of his duties and in fact was blocked from doing so.[35]

The anthropomorphic suffering that the corporation has come to embody on symbolic stages is strictly tied to the blind interests it serves, and it is only in the formal framework of the law that it can express that suffering, such as in suits claiming "defamation" for attacks on its "reputation." It then claims "damages" calculated in dollars to provide tangible consistency to its fictitious internal pain. Several courts around the world still largely accept such suits, granting substance to what from the point of view of common sense is clearly a hallucination.

We have reached such a degree of perversion that all the subjects of the system, from employees to the CEO, struggle to satisfy the economic and legal expectations of

Frankenstein corporations rather than having these social institutions suit the inclinations of historical subjects.

If, in this anthropomorphic symbolism conceived by the law and imposed by force in the name of public order, the American federal state were to consider itself as a "person," the book one would wish it to consult with some urgency is *Otherwise Than Being* by Emmanuel Lévinas. It would then meditate on this: whoever tries to define what he is in essence comes to understand that what he is does not go beyond him as though it were a foreign thing detached from itself—a pure definition, a simple construction, or a "constitution"— that one would merely indicate as being from a distance the strictly conceptualized equivalent of the quintessence of the self. It would ask itself: does the essence of the public subjectivity that I embody, in the person of the state, still mean anything other than what is agreed and folded into its mere formulation—"we the people"—and the vulgar extent of its existence dedicated in priority to psychopathic corporations? It would agree that language supposed to grasp the essence of the subjectivity of the state itself can in no way constitute an object distinct from the historical institution that expresses its existence. It would seek to have essence in the form of the state find in history a real significance—that form of the state—seeking constantly to complete itself in time as it evolves. It would fear that in its person, the state, in the way the constitution says, presents itself as divided in relation to the functions it performs in reality once it has become the instrument of capital and its "people" are made up of corporate "persons." It would recognize its sudden vanity in openly claiming opposition to tax havens once those claims allow themselves to be reified as decorations in a detached realm. Having become an object in the service of powers that are beyond it, the person of the state would recognize that in the light of the essential definition by which its constitution presents it on the stage of meaning, it is unrecognizable because it has turned out to be so violent and blind toward its own—"we the people"—in the realm of power relations. The fictitious "persons" that are corporations have reduced me to the rank of their instrument, it would conclude, by making the formal text in which I clothe myself strictly ornamental. In the words of Emmanuel Lévinas: "Can he that looks place himself outside of the Absolute, and the look withdraw from the event of being by hollowing out the fold of inwardness, in which knowledge is deposited, accumulates, and is formulated? . . . Being's essence designates nothing that could be a nameable content, a thing, event, or action; it names this mobility of the immobile, this multiplication of the identical, this diastasis of the punctual, this lapse."[36]

The question is this: if the person of the state persists today as a person without definition that renews itself over time, but in considering "the people" as a people of corporations threatened with harm by the subaltern workers, employees, and managers that they subjugate, is this a renewal of something identical or a phenomenon of corruption? Out of a state ruled by law issuing from a popular revolution has arisen in history an entity for the defense of corporations, harboring within itself regulatory havens that are internationally harmful. To what extent can the "lapse" of such a transformation still claim to renew the "identical"? Although the philosophical question may lead us far afield, is that not because in history, with blinding clarity, the question arises of the denaturing of the revolutionary project of a state ruled by law into a monstrosity that calls for a revolution?

10

THE COMEDY OF THE
"FIGHT AGAINST TAX HAVENS"
WHO'S AFRAID OF THE RULE OF LAW

For many reasons, governments can no longer give the impression that they still tolerate massive tax evasion, proliferating crime networks, drug money transformed into real estate or industrial investments with a few mouse clicks, international development funds diverted into numbered accounts, or mercenaries and arms dealers financed by oil and mining interests stirring up bloody conflict.

Oddly, judges were the first to take action. In 1996, seven European magistrates met in Switzerland, and with the assistance of the journalist Denis Robert and the publisher Laurent Beccaria, launched L'Appel de Genève.[1] They denounced the national borders and banking secrecy that prevented them from piecing together the complex financial arrangements new criminal forces had developed. It took them years to obtain judicial information about a transaction conducted in less than five minutes.

At the turn of the millennium, tax havens came to the fore as a political problem. A plethora of independent documents were published demonstrating their harmful effects in many areas of social activity. The international organizations Global Witness,[2] Oxfam International,[3] Transparency International,[4] Survie France,[5] various national branches of the Association for the Taxation of Financial Transactions for the Aid of Citizens (Attac), and the French Magistrates Union[6] have each in turn denounced the political corruption, arms traffic, mercenary forces, state crimes, counterfeiting, and transport of dangerous elements or protected resources authorized or facilitated by tax havens. At the same time, the English-speaking world published books such as *Offshore World* by Ronen Palan and *Wages of Crime* by R.T. Naylor; critical organizations were established, such as the Tax Justice Network in Great Britain and the Plateforme française sur les paradis fiscaux et judiciares; researchers frequently referred to the role of offshore centers in finance and crime, including Alain Labrousse on the question of drugs,[7] Richard Poulin on the sex industry,[8] and François Lille on the shipping industry;[9] and Robert and Ernest Backes were about to publish *Révélation$* on the offshore activities of clearinghouses.[10]

These were the circumstances in which the first blacklists from international bodies appeared in 2000, stigmatizing tax havens on specific points for their lack of cooperation with tax and judicial investigators from legitimate states. The OECD, representing the major financial powers, focused on the problem of tax evasion;[11] the Financial Stability Forum (FSF), supported by the IMF, considered stock market speculation and insider trading;[12] and the Financial Action Task Force (FATF), which had been investigating the drug traffic since 1989, turned its attention to "terrorist" activities linked to international banking.[13]

The OECD anticipated some real progress against the tax havens on its blacklist, by demanding, for example, the lifting of bank secrecy on the real owners of companies and trusts located there, or in limitations on offshore assets or the number of entities with no real activity that could be established in them. This failed to take into account the 2000 American election. Just as Ronald Reagan in 1980 had disregarded the report that Richard A. Gordon had presented to President Jimmy Carter at the very end of his mandate to assess the magnitude of the offshore phenomenon, the Bush administration put a stop to the process.[14] At the same time, Barbados, the unofficial tax haven for Canada, took the lead in a group of Caribbean nations under the banner of the International Tax Investment Organization to fight against the OECD initiative.[15]

The process became pathetic and dealt only with the transparency of operators and the exchange of information. The result was an inconsequential policy of "naming and shaming," and then the list became practically pure white, with the targeted tax havens promising to respect appropriate requirements to get off the list. Thereafter, although foreign judges and investigators were able to obtain information, this was only in exceptional circumstances.

To be crossed off the blacklist, offshore jurisdictions used methods as opaque as those targeted by the authorities' initiatives. Bermuda was a notable example: the archipelago went through the challenge unscathed not because it respected the criteria to attain the objectives but because it had an international lobby.

The same thing was true for Switzerland. Using its power as a member of the OECD, it avoided being placed on the blacklist even though it conformed perfectly to the defining criteria the organization had provided for offshore centers. Mark Peith, a Swiss expert on the fight against money laundering, says, "Swiss laws against money laundering are impressive, but there is a serious crisis in applying them. The Money Laundering Reporting Office and the Financial Market Supervisory Authority have not worked. There are few resources compared to the role of the financial sector. Ten people to supervise one-third of the world's private banking! That's just not serious."[16] Convictions since the law was put in place can be counted on the fingers of one hand.

Through some perverse effects, the blacklist, like the gray list that made its appearance in 2009, even helped consolidate the offshore phenomenon. Most striking was the legitimation of any tax haven that was not or was no longer on the list. Not being on the blacklist is now a commercial argument, and it is possible to become an *equitable* tax haven with little effort.

The FATF revised its blacklist downward without revealing the principles governing this change. "This leads one to question the standards used, which, apparently, were in the end incorporated by the reputedly most opaque financial centers, enabling them to avoid public identification," note Thierry Godefroy and Pierre Lascoumes.[17] And the FSF had developed management criteria that went along the lines of international conventions governing liability and the supervision of banking and financial activity, which prevented none of the economic excesses revealed a decade later. Hedge funds are particularly controversial. These risk investment funds registered in tax havens are subject to control by no established government.

Supported by the G7 and the IMF, the FSF published

"good practice principles," always subject to "voluntary" enforcement by offshore players. The actual list of countries stigmatized by the FSF disappeared in 2003. Superintendent of Financial Institutions Canada John Palmer, who had been charged with establishing it, had automatically excluded the offshore centers located in the United Kingdom (London) and the United States (Delaware).[18] The list was established in complete secrecy. The FSF itself has its headquarters in Basel, Switzerland, a tax haven.

The European Union also found itself in the hot seat. The authors of L'Appel de Genève had initially challenged it by denouncing "the Europe of numbered accounts and money laundering machines . . . used to recycle money from drugs, terrorism, sects, corruption, and the Mafia." The judges from Belgium, Spain, France, Italy, and Switzerland declared it to be "urgent to abolish outmoded protectionism in police and judicial matters" in Europe.[19] But when the European Union attacked its internal offshore problem, only marginal fraudsters paid the price. In the 2000s, the European Union hit a wall when it tried to breach banking secrecy as it was practiced, notably, in Luxembourg. On the pretext of the principle of competition, Luxembourg's representatives pointed out that any constraint imposed on them would favor the rival financial center of Switzerland. There then began an absurd diplomatic battle between Luxembourg and Switzerland over who would be the first to abolish its rules governing banking secrecy, whereas neither had any interest in giving in on anything. All that came out of these exchanges was a paradoxical global tax imposed in those countries on money deposited in their banks by foreign *individuals*. Thus, between 2004 and 2006, the European Union collected withholding tax equivalent to 15 percent of the total deposits of nonresidents, a rate that increased to 20 percent for 2007–9 and reached 35 percent on January 1, 2010.

"The measure is aimed at limiting the exclusive use for tax purposes of the free circulation of capital and the free offer of services guaranteed to physical persons Europe-wide," according to official statements.[20] But it meant primarily that banking secrecy in the European Union was financed by those who needed it the least, individuals, and not by offshore investors as a whole, including banks and private companies, among other "corporate persons."

Thus legitimated, at the expense of their smallest beneficiaries, the tax havens of Europe could undermine the principle of the application of law and taxation in Europe and in addition, through these agreements, benefit from political recognition. This recognition was important to them. Whereas they had had to face international criticism since the 1990s, Luxembourg and Switzerland relied respectively on their membership in the EU and the OECD, rather than making common cause with the International Tax and Investment Organization (ITIO), thereby laying claim to the status of *respectable* tax havens compared to other jurisdictions with shady reputations like the Caribbean. The purpose of banking secrecy is not merely to encrypt data but also to preserve the honor of those who use it. This has not kept Swiss bankers from recommending to their clients that they open accounts through shell corporations created in the tax havens of the Caribbean, preferably in Panama and the British Virgin Islands, which have signed treaties on double taxation with Switzerland.[21] In fact, 50 percent of the international financial transactions signed in Switzerland involve another of the world's offshore jurisdictions.

The cost of this international agreement with the European Union was minimal for countries such as Luxembourg and Switzerland. It nonetheless provoked hostility from right-wing economists. Grégoire Duhamel said of the trial of strength between Luxembourg and the EU, "Taxation enables the maintenance for the moment of the principle of banking secrecy, that a number of European countries dream of seeing removed under the pressure of their leftwing electorate." Non-"left-wing" Europe, barricaded in "havens" of all kinds, once again chose to reverse the terms of the debate. Valentin Petkantchin of the Institut Économique Molinari wrote in the *Financial Times*, "The European Commission seems to recognise no limits in its drive to impose tax harmonisation across Europe," as though he did not recognize that what was at stake was not on the contrary establishing limits where there were none. For him, the only "rights" that count are those of free competition and free enterprise. The European citizen is seen not as part of a whole on which he is dependent but as an individual endowed with resources absolutely unconnected with his social context. As a result, the European tax measure, "if it succeeds, will hurt not only the Swiss but all taxpayers in Europe. Tax competition gives you—the entrepreneur or citizen—the opportunity to escape fiscal pressure from your government by moving to jurisdictions with more favourable tax regimes. It gives strong incentives for all governments to lower taxes, allowing taxpayers to keep more of their money and making markets less distorted."[22] A lovely Europe in prospect, with global dumping driven and accentuated by the offshore centers.

Incidentally, the European Union imposed other measures against Luxembourg that affected only outmoded management entities. The EU abolished the "1929 holding companies," leaving intact more flexible and even less restrictive forms of incorporation, such as financial holding companies (*sociétés de participation financière*, or Soparfi), subject to low or virtually zero levels of taxation in the Grand Duchy and easily accessible from the thirty-eight legitimate states that had already signed dubious treaties with Luxembourg on "double taxation."[23] This means that the assets of a holding company can reside in Luxembourg subject to a highly advantageous rate of taxation and eventually be "repatriated" to their country of origin without being taxed a "second time," as though what was really due had been paid the first time. This measure was thus merely symbolic, because a "1929 holding company" only had to change itself into a Soparfi. Luxembourg already "has 15,000 of these holding companies, which account for a capital of €21 billion and pay only minimal taxes (1 percent of subscribed capital). These companies guarantee their owners anonymity and allow for the issuance of bearer shares," according to Godefroy and Lascoumes.[24]

This perversion of tax laws, as the corporate lawyer Grégoire Duhamel was pleased to point out, was expressed essentially in "instruments for the management of private fortunes." As a result, this attack on the management of public resources has provoked, in his words, "the anger of critics of every stripe."[25]

In 2009, the OECD and a G20 subject to increasing media attention worked officially to eradicate the offshore problem, but in reality to circumscribe it so that it remained the privilege of a well-defined minority. The so-called international community had some new reasons to tighten the screws, because traditional states had showered billions on a financial world that had been playing at sorcerer's apprentice with other people's money. But when states already largely indebted to the banks lend money to those same banks, it is easy to see that they are eager to find sources of revenue. Offshore reserves turned out to be a solution, no doubt provisional. But in reality the fight "against tax havens" and "the end of banking secrecy" proclaimed by the media are limited to occasional and circumscribed surveillance solely of tax evasion. And even so, it is conducted within such limits that it leaves out of account significant areas of cheating. To this day, in fact, no public measure claiming to "fight against tax havens" has done anything but approach the offshore problem marginally. The mobilization of law-governed states in the spring and summer of 2009 was directed primarily at concentrating offshore assets within a narrow compass and in fewer extraterritorial financial centers. Too many inconsistencies and anomalies surfaced in these public actions for any other view to be possible. For example, the OECD, supported by the G20 countries, that summer placed a certain number of offshore jurisdictions on its blacklist, then again removed the names (and the meaning of the list). They then established a gray list including tax havens as different as Austria, Bermuda, and Vanuatu, demanding that they sign twelve conventions for judicial cooperation with foreign countries based on OECD conventions. These promises of cooperation carried little weight. In the eyes of cynical investors and bankers, they merely confirmed the purely masking function of a ponderously bureaucratic and ineffective state.

The financial arrangements made to facilitate money laundering that were in question could be so complex (there was talk of hundreds of shell companies in several different jurisdictions to camouflage money laundering operations or the regulation of various forms of illegal trafficking) that a judge or an investigator from a law-governed state could not justify an indictment until secrecy was breached. And secrecy was breached precisely only when a judge was in a position to document the reasons for his suspicions. The chairman of the French parliamentary commission on money laundering, Vincent Peillon, was outraged:

> How many judges, in cases involving not benign and banal tax evasion, but transnational crime, have been confronted with situations in which, not knowing the exact number of the account, they were halted in their investigations by the rigidity of bankers and national judicial authorities? Carried to extremes, the refusal to authorize investigations of this kind means granting assistance only when the evidence is in the possession of the investigators! In other words, the ultimate safety mechanism for the fraudster is the absence of judicial cooperation.[26]

As in other places, offshore, some are more equal than others. The G20 has its protégés. The OECD's blacklist and later its gray list completely omit tax havens dependent on the regimes of Great Britain, Canada, and the United States. London and the British dependencies such as the Channel Islands or some of the Caribbean islands are conspicuous by their absence, as are Delaware and offshore Caribbean outposts closely tied to U.S. finance. But corporate lawyers and other specialists in tax cheating still today publicly sing the praises of the discretion of these financial centers and the opacity that defines them.

The City of London is a tax haven that attracts very

large flows of bank transactions. About one-half of the total sum of bank loans and international deposits in the world's financial institutions are found in tax havens: 40 percent of these flows converge on London and are protected, as in any tax haven, by banking secrecy and a tax rate of practically zero.[27] It is impossible to measure the volume of transactions attributable to the fact that London is a tax haven and those that are not. The London financial district, a veritable offshore principality within the state, leading the state rather than the converse, rarely cooperates with foreign judicial authorities and provides no concrete follow-up to its promises of international self-regulation.[28] The situation was so problematic that Vincent Peillon, chairman of a commission on tax havens at the turn of the millennium, titled his report: *The City of London, Gibraltar, and the Crown Dependencies: Offshore Centers, Sanctuaries for Dirty Money.*[29] London embodies the deep interconnections between legitimate and criminal finance, which can no longer be distinguished. The very use of the terms "legitimate" and "criminal" has lost all meaning.

Canada similarly goes without mention, although it protects domestically a mining industry that is challenged around the world for the environmental, political, and social harm it has caused.

As for Delaware, it is at the very least surprising that it has not been subjected to any international pressure, although the IRS conducted a major legal battle in 2009 against UBS because it had encouraged individuals in American territory to evade taxes by using the Swiss financial center.

One may ask, as José Gayoso of Attac has not hesitated to do, whether Washington is not taking advantage of the pretext of the alleged fight against tax havens to "fleece Switzerland" and eliminate a major competitor in the offshore capital market. Gayoso points out that the tiny Cayman Islands hold twice the amount of deposits of American citizens as the richest state of the union, California. The United States and the United Kingdom—backed by a French president who is close to the United States and a friend of the Bush family, and supported in its political conquests by the Canadian Anglophile Paul Desmarais—put pressure on all tax havens except their own. They agreed to grant their protégés "a certificate of tax haven virtue." "The big winners in the G20 are the Anglo-Saxon tax havens and as a result Anglo-Saxon finance," Gayoso writes.[30]

The retired Swiss judge Bernard Betossa was surprised at the absence of China (Macao) and the United Kingdom (the city of London and many British dependencies). In an article about Betossa, David Serrenay writes, "When you see countries like England, for example, get off practically scot-free, when you know that England is in practice one of the least cooperative countries, in tax matters as well as in matters of financial crime strictly speaking, you may fear that the exercise will turn out to be an illusion, putting small states in their place and not really troubling the larger ones."[31] In his book, Bertossa evokes the strictly political pressures that explain why the authorities stick to formal criteria with little impact.[32] His judgment on the gaps in the process is merciless; he considers the criteria in question "fanciful," especially because equally "fanciful" states can sign agreements for judicial cooperation that will have no consequences. Bertossa has spent his life pointing out manifestations of hypocrisy by representatives of legitimate states as well as by agents of tax havens. He recalls that France, in the person of Jacques Toubon, had officially criticized Switzerland for not adopting banking secrecy. He also attacks the Swiss banks that armed themselves with a kind of banking secrecy squared when, fearing a strengthening of Swiss legislation on financial crime, they sent certain hot accounts to their own Caribbean branches: "A Swiss bank could not possibly rely on banking secrecy supposedly binding on a foreign branch to refuse to produce documents in its own possession."[33]

Hence, more questions than answers arise from the protected areas that have been deployed as a consequence of the OECD lists: to what extent will the principles of the fight against tax havens be applied? Why stop at the borders of Anglo-Saxon regimes? Why not also mention such notorious tax havens as Hong Kong and Macao?

To what levels will the fight be extended? Why is the fight against political corruption not a priority? Why do American anti-money-laundering laws sanction improper transfers of funds abroad only for a narrow range of reasons?

How far should control be carried? Will *all* drug traffickers finally be pursued? Will there be a focus not just on individuals or a few cowboy investors held responsible for the economic crisis, but on the multinationals that pillage the South through pernicious influence peddling and violent predatory operations? On the major investors that are literally outside the law? Will the IMF and the World Bank be challenged for their complacent support of industrial and financial players unworthy of trust?

Will there be any inquiry into the unfortunate direct consequences for the populations of exotic offshore islands exposed to the massive influx of corporate lawyers who have come to enable their clients to profit from these mythical money havens? Customs duties in tax havens have soared because that is often the only form of taxation.[34] Yet certain poor countries anticipate establishing offshore arrangements to attract law firms, banks, and private capital. The system forces or encourages those who suffer from it to adopt its own measures.

Despite all these reservations, all it took was a few reactivated fetishes (the OECD lists), a few fiery sentences against tax havens at the G20 summit, and Switzerland marginally eroding bank secrecy for the United States in the framework of a new treaty on double taxation for irresponsible media voices to see "the end of banking secrecy" and of tax havens.[35]

Of course, there was some real symbolic progress in the summer of 2009. Switzerland was forced to agree to review the sacrosanct principle of banking secrecy with respect to the American giant in the framework of a new treaty on double taxation. It also agreed to make the accounts of some 4,400 Americans accessible. And most important, an international challenge was posed to the legal definitions in force in jurisdictions of convenience of terms such as tax "evasion" and tax "fraud." We know, for example, that Switzerland had previously promised to provide information on cases of "fraud" only by virtue of *its* definition of the term. The new agreement for judicial cooperation that it signed with the United States should force it to adopt the American definition.

But at the same time that they were heralding "the end of tax havens," Western media were reporting spectacular frauds that relied on offshore financial services. This type of fraud is the work of a new breed of white-collar criminals who have proliferated by using the principle of the Ponzi scheme: these fake investors claim to invest the money entrusted to them, but they keep it for themselves. The "proceeds" that they distribute regularly, falsely claiming profitable investments, inspire enough trust for new customers to hand over their funds. As long as the investor finds new recruits, the game goes on. And the author of this hoax grows prodigiously wealthy along the way—until an economic crisis drives most investors to suddenly withdraw their assets, which turn out to be desperately lacking. Three spectacular cases involving offshore jurisdictions made headlines: Bernard Madoff on an international scale, Allen Stanford in the United States, and Earl Jones in Canada.

Madoff, a former chairman of NASDAQ, defrauded the financial elite itself of some $60 billion through intermediaries operating in Luxembourg. A study by journalists Romain Gubert and Emmanuel Saint-Martin reveals that European brokers associated with Madoff handled their funds through accounts in BNP-Paribas. Independent of the question of banking secrecy, tax havens accept foreign capital with no inquiry as to its nature: Luxembourg "rolls out the red carpet for anyone who has money. A SICAV [mutual fund] can be created administratively in a few days, and be officially approved in a few weeks, whereas in France, the same procedures take an enormous amount of time," Gubert and Saint-Martin found.[36]

The Texan Allen Stanford is alleged to have extracted some $9 billion from investors and savers by orchestrating a fraud "through his bank, the Stanford International Bank, headquartered in Antigua, with the help of its managers and a financial regulator on the island," reported Tabussam Zakaria in *Le Devoir*.[37] Stanford himself was the primary figure in the tax haven's banking industry and sat on its "supervisory" bodies. His activities are also alleged to have included the laundering of drug money.[38]

Meanwhile in Canada, several presumed cases of fraud

came out in the summer of 2009. Earl Jones was alleged to have deceived savers of all kinds by extracting from them $50 million Canadian. At this point it is believed that $500,000 is in an account in Bermuda: "The trustee wants to secure an order from the government of this tax haven to determine if there are still funds in the account in question," according to Radio-Canada.ca.[39] Two other presumed cases of Ponzi schemes popped up during this period, one concerning a firm registered in the Bahamas.[40]

This all took place around the same time as this series of raids in the United States: "Forty local officials and five rabbis were arrested in New York area suburbs in the dismantling of a network of corruption that reached as far as Israel and Switzerland. . . . The authorities accuse the arrested men of corruption, extortion, money laundering, and organ trafficking," reported *Le Devoir*.[41]

Nothing is settled, even in the pages that tell us that everything is settled. Anyone who speaks of the "end of tax havens" has not taken into consideration their numerous and problematic purposes, which have not yet received the attention they deserve from the public authorities.

The measures imposed on tax havens are unlikely to limit their operations, except possibly in Switzerland, which has come out of its battle with the American empire diminished. Methods of control tied to the promises made in order to be taken off the black and gray lists are practically nonexistent. They are formalities relying on the political smoke and mirrors of self-regulation. Vincent Peillon shows all its imposture in his book *Les Milliards noirs du blanchiment*: not even one-third of the London banks provided data on money laundering in 2000, supposedly a year of heightened scrutiny. In

Switzerland, no banker was so enthusiastic as to denounce a customer suspected of money laundering. It was better to play dumb and run the risk of one day paying a paltry fine.[42] Law-governed states will continue to come up against Swiss banking secrecy, because the country lifts that secrecy only when it facilitates criminal activities, according to its own criteria for evaluating the criminal character of those activities. Because tax evasion is not a crime in Switzerland, a request from a foreign examining magistrate in that area would be rejected. "For the libertarian-conservative camp, tax evasion becomes a right once the state imposes a tax burden that is too heavy for their taste," writes Sylvain Besson. Not to mention that in Switzerland, "companies themselves cannot be held criminally liable," but are subject only to the authority of the Swiss Bankers Association, which "inflicts" fines that never exceed 500,000 Swiss francs, and then it does not publish the names of the guilty parties.[43]

The crooks and robbers of finance have learned to adapt with ease to the new methods of control. Criminal organizations use straw men to open accounts under false names, concealing the real account holders. Not to mention offshore jurisdictions that, regardless of statements of principle, compete against one another to attract the billions in dirty money to be laundered.

The attacks of September 11, 2001, led the American authorities to strengthen control over the banking sector to fight against the money of the "terrorists," particularly in connection with the links between American financial institutions with "fictitious" foreign banks. But once again, the banks avoided practical application of these statements of principle. How could a bank go through the daily flows and intercept transactions affecting accounts held in shadow banks practicing money laundering, financial fraud, or tax evasion? Marie-Christine Dupuis-Danon notes, "It is difficult to go beyond a theoretical check for the existence of anti-laundering procedures, because an individual study of the corresponding bank's clients would incur delays and methods incompatible with the daily volume of banking transactions."[44] And who would be seriously motivated to diminish the financial flows that banking interests are always seeking to increase?

It is therefore hardly surprising that the rate of failure in anti-money-laundering efforts is 99.9 percent.[45] The enforcement of anti-money-laundering laws enables the United States to recover $250 million annually, whereas the Treasury Department estimates the sums laundered at $250 billion.

According to Raymond W. Baker, the duplicity of "legitimate states" is beyond question: "The fact is that laundered proceeds of drug trafficking, racketeering, corruption, and terrorism tag along with other forms of dirty money to which the United States and Europe extend a welcoming hand. . . . Western banks solicit, transfer, accumulate, and manage dirty money in the trillions of dollars, raking in hundreds of billions every year."[46] Baker, a former major international trader who now works as a consultant in Washington to save capitalism from the moral cancer that is eating away at it, affirms that most international meetings of first-rank financial players focus much more on ways of getting around anti-laundering laws than on ways of applying them.

The arbitrary way these measures are enforced raises the question of the conflicts of interest confronting the political representatives who manage the lists through international bodies, determine which "terrorist" will have his banking secrecy removed, and for which honest major creator of jobs it can be maintained.

An investigation conducted late in the last decade explains the pitiful results of international financial controls by the fact that governments loudly proclaim promises whose application is in reality turned over to their banks. This "public-private partnership" usually leads to "cosmetic" enforcement of the regulations. When it comes to supervision, the banks formally aim at particular goals that only partially overlap with those of governments. They work to foster their own interests: "With regard to anti-laundering, the principal risk that financial establishments want to master is less that of an illegal transaction or a lawbreaking customer than the danger of a public challenge for not conforming to legal and professional norms," according to Favarel-Garrigues, Godefroy, and Lascoumes.[47] Covering themselves becomes the banks' principal concern, so they multiply statements of doubt in contexts where they are not justified in order to discharge their responsibility. These are "umbrella statements." This "shield" has the perverse effect of completely clogging the system of supervision, which is deficient in more than one respect. Because of exclusive reliance on the legal criterion, explains R. Kent Weaver, "this type of politics covers actions with no great ambition or real program, conducted at a slow speed, with no clear commitment or reference to a coherent value system, politically poorly directed, and in which professional strategies and routines end up running the show. These are in a sense minimal programs of action aimed at avoiding hard conflicts and above all public disgrace harmful to reputation."[48] Dupuis-Danon also remarks on the absence of critical thought in the application of these protocols. Banks apply this criterion more to cash deposits made in their establishments than to "inter-bank transfers" involving "sometimes sizeable sums of dirty money prelaundered in other countries."[49]

Technology and computers make it possible for the institution to fetishize actions that accomplish nothing. Statements expressing suspicion of one or another transaction often lead nowhere—suspicion is not proof. And qualitatively, absolutely nothing is settled. It remains very difficult to identify a money-laundering operation that, when well conducted, has all the appearances of an ordinary transaction. The transactions in question are not criminal in themselves but are connected to activities that are. They are therefore not only hard to detect technically but also hard to define legally. The technology-worshipping gestures surrounding banks' fight against money laundering are thus of little help in containing the offshore problem. In these circumstances, tax havens retain all their prerogatives and those that assert they are applying anti-laundering rules are given the title of *equitable* tax havens, while the underlying problem remains unaffected.

This is all the clearer because these anti-laundering measures, although negotiated internationally, are applied on the national level at the exclusive discretion of the local authorities. From level to level, from international circles to central national governments to various domestic services and then to the institutions themselves, or even depending on the professions and services that take charge of the question within each company, the principles and objectives of anti-money-laundering measures are constantly reinterpreted, circumscribed, modified, and diminished.

Banks thus try to save face in front of their respective judicial and national institutions, which attribute to the banks an unnatural oversight function, creating a conflict of interest. It is the bankers who must formally distinguish between a tax fraud that is "legitimate" and one that is not. Indeed, studies assert that one employee out of two, subjected to contradictory demands and the imperative of a high volume of transactions, generally violates institutional rules to achieve his goals. Because of their self-interested position, bankers are still looking for the distinction between clean and dirty financial flows, whereas the problem on the contrary now consists of the total confusion between the two.

This approach confirms the intuition of the philosopher Michel Surya: anti-money-laundering programs and the emphasis their discourse places on dirty money, its illegitimacy, and its harmful consequences are aimed less at attacking an evil than at creating clean money elsewhere—giving rise to the very idea of money that is clean once it is not dirty. Anti-laundering programs launder money as such. The height of perversion is that the scaffolding of "ethical," "equitable," "transparent," and "clean" measures tends to absolve the activity of capital once it is no longer or not yet stigmatized. Minds are then forced to conceive of it as being regulated, governed, just, free, and even enviable, curiously for lack of receiving a fair share of it. "Capital knows this: that it will hold on to all power, that it will even increase in power, only if it ritually submits to the appearance that it is shared," writes Surya. By "proving that there are henceforth no more illegal profits, one would provide the truly moral proof that money could be *equal* by means of the very movement that made it become *legal*."[50]

11

TWO-HEADED EUROPE

The most optimistic will say that the adhesion of tax havens such as Malta and Cyprus to the European Union will force them to "democratize." This means taking literally the claims of states to follow principles of "justice" and "democracy" and forgetting that "tax havens" are the offspring of these law-governed states. It is true that the statutes governing offshore companies in Malta have been changed to some degree. The island republic had to amend "a certain number of provisions" of its tax system to prevent challenges, and it undertook on its own to "clean up a bit of the most dubious fringes of its fleet": ships more than twenty-five years old will no longer be authorized and oversight measures will be strengthened. But François Lille and Raphaël Baumler have already expressed doubt that the companies to which that oversight has been subcontracted really have the resources, the mandate, and the will to apply those measures rigorously.[1]

The most pessimistic will understand that this interference of interests hostile to national law within the European

Union itself allows the notion of "convenience" to use EU bodies to strengthen its position in Europe as well as in international forums. It has, for example, been possible to legalize the ever greater and more consequential geographical distance that separates ships' flags of convenience from their real home ports. As a result and by force of circumstance, the offshore "laws" that provide neither more nor less for the absence of laws and the radical impossibility of prohibiting anyone from doing anything will cover ships wherever they sail by making these "laws" valid everywhere. This is already the case, because in international law, "the flag state has authority over the ship at all times and places. It issues permission to sail and sets the conditions to be respected for that, and the economic and social conditions of its activity, and the ship's owner is subject to its jurisdiction," explain Lille and Baumler.[2]

The European Union epitomizes all by itself the duplicity of traditional states with regard to tax havens. The two legal and jurisdictional systems that coexist in the EU, those of law-governed states and those of offshore jurisdictions such as Austria, Belgium, Cyprus, Luxembourg, Malta, and the United Kingdom (the City of London), constitute and define it, making of it a historical contradiction. European "Union," to be sure, but between what and what?

Judge Jean de Maillard has constantly thought about this paradox in his considerations on the offshore question. A fundamental contradiction runs through his writings, attributable not to his thinking but to a characteristic of the time. On one side, in *Le Marché fait sa loi*, he substantiates the argument that law-governed states now facing a structural "crisis" are totally overwhelmed by the criminal entities proliferating offshore:

"Formal" society, in all of its political, economic, and social components, is now intertwined inextricably with the criminal economy. One can no longer speak globally of a legal society on one side, even one in the process of shrinking, and a criminal society on the other. We are facing a criminal-legal society all of whose components, criminal and legal, are interwoven together. All these reasons make the crisis of nation-states and of modern political forms irreversible, based as they are on the will to promote continuous social integration and rationalization.[3]

But on the other, he has told the magazine *Jeune Afrique/l'Intelligent* that, formally, it would take just a stroke of the pen to have legitimate states make offshore centers disappear:

Tax havens are only illusions in the international financial system and exist only because the major industrialized countries need them. We are swimming in hypocrisy: we act as though those countries were independent and as though we must not interfere in their affairs, whereas three-fourths of them are dependencies of the United States or Great Britain. They would not exist if it was decided that they not exist; it's as simple as that.[4]

International public bodies actively busy themselves overseeing offshore activity at the same time as they denounce it on public platforms.

An example is provided by two international clearinghouses located in Europe, Clearstream and Euroclear. While the public treasuries of legitimate European states suffer

considerable losses because of tax evasion that feeds criminal circuits absolutely contrary to democratic principles, the
European Union finds itself overseeing the various activities
of the tax havens that make it up, exactly as though they were
merely economic networks among others. It thus played the
role of mediator in the dispute that broke out in the middle
of the last decade between Euroclear and Clearstream,
housed by the two European tax havens of Belgium and
Luxembourg. Following the publication of the explosive book
by Denis Robert and Ernest Backes on Clearstream—the
journalist and the former company employee dissected its
structure to explain how it was possible to record practically
in real time legal and criminal international transactions
conducted both in legitimate states and in tax havens—
the clearinghouse reorganized and found a new owner, not
a consortium of banks but the Deutsche Börse. This posed
competition problems. The Deutsche Börse, which owns and
manages the Frankfurt stock exchange, of course enables its
clearinghouse Clearstream to have access to the German financial market, but as a consequence hampers its competitor
Euroclear. It has therefore become difficult for Euroclear to
record transactions occurring in that market. This is when
the European Union intervened, but solely as a technician,
to ensure that nothing would hinder the principle of "free
competition" between the two clearinghouses. Its aim was
to establish the rules of the game that should prevail in the
matter.[5]

But the intervention of the European Union was expected on an entirely different level. When Denis Robert
and Ernest Backes published *Révélation$*, a book that earns
its title, on the presumed crime-engendering functions of
this financial "supertool," the European Union decided to

allow the debate to focus on the problem of "defamation," rather than to examine the question politically. Somehow, the European Commission in Brussels, and hence the sovereign nation-states that determine its policies, in the name of competition, authorized and oversaw two entities dedicated to lubricating a wide variety of trafficking that these legitimate states had in principle vowed to block and control. This public oversight was thus paradoxical in two respects, and coincides with the assessments of Jean de Maillard. Not only does a public body sanction and supervise the activities of this mysterious financial machine, but the managers of offshore operations that direct and use it have felt the need to turn to the public arbitration of Europe to settle their dispute.

12

THE REDUCTION OF DEMOCRACIES
TO LEGALISTIC STATES

While tax havens welcome bankers, investors, insurers, industrialists, traffickers, shipowners, and lawyers wishing to
develop their billion-dollar activities free from rules of law,
legitimate states find themselves economically dependent
on the investments of these very players. Although those investments are often money-laundering operations, states act
humble and express gratitude: they no longer assert law as
a political principle but put themselves at the service of a
law adapted to financial interests. These states, subject to the
paltry proceeds of investments made in their jurisdictions by
offshore investors (who are thus politically unattached), more
closely resemble bailiffs managing the institutions of corporate law than bodies asserting the values of a system that can
legitimately lay claim to the word "justice." This submission
to the interests of the stronger, this state clientelism made
into a method, this capitulation disguised as a triumph, this
"end of history" accepted as science, this denial of thought
repeated like the ticking of a clock, this management of

public life, this mediocrity required of holders of "responsible" positions, is all subsumed under the dispiriting term "governance," which is rapidly replacing the historically meaningful terms "democracy" and "politics." Those in positions of authority in the state no longer hesitate to present themselves, even in forums over which they preside, as "partners," although the themes under discussion, programs at issue, and measures being deliberated are all fixed by the economic sovereigns who have the power to affect reality.

"Governance" means management replacing politics, a large industrial development destroying the local economy, expertise obliterating public thinking, accounting "proof" disqualifying people's knowledge, the monumental megalomania of the powerful destroying common sense. Finally, it means the legitimate state giving way to the legalistic state, a state entirely devoted to the administration of legal and bureaucratic arrangements at the service of decisions, programs, and eventually a history largely beyond its control.

This is what remains of public authorities in a political world that concentrates the prerogatives of the powerful offshore. From the point of view of justice, the legalistic state presents itself to the investor as a mere officer of the court; from the fiscal perspective, it subsidizes industry rather than taxing it, and the state borrows funds from industry to function. Taxation targets essentially the personnel trained at the expense of the state hired by the sovereign investor, along with the investor's incidental expenditures. From the diplomatic point of view, the legalistic state is a broker who strives to promote on the world market the natural resources abounding in its territory and the infrastructure it has built so it could be pillaged. From the political point of view, the state is no longer concerned with sovereign law and focuses primarily on its security, that is, the defense of the arrangements that enable it to offer its priceless services to capital. It transforms its citizens into licensed "representatives of civil society," whom it often appoints itself, and turns its public associations into "nongovernmental" organizations that it nonetheless finances in order to restrict political discussion to a circle of initiates able to use expert discourse to discredit anyone who has not mastered the codes.

The public representative accepts this confinement to the restricted prerogatives of the legalistic state because his client, the investor, finances his political party and his own election campaigns precisely through tax havens. This was illustrated explosively by a trial that brought to light the oil company Elf's secret African funds, as the Canadian commission charged with investigating the secret financing of the Liberal Party in the mid-1990s might have done if only it had been given the right to conduct detailed investigations outside Canadian territory.

Financial players themselves help draft the laws promulgated by the state through the lobbies they create and finance. In Europe, the European Round Table brings together powerful multinationals and has succeeded in promoting huge continental projects requiring large-scale investments and even cultural transformations.[1] Lobbying firms formally registered in the capitals of the North are often close to the parties in power. Nor is it unusual for former ministers or elected officials to work as lobbyists in the pay of major financial groups. These pressure groups are formidable because they blur the exclusive relationship that, in principle, should join political representatives to the people who choose them. Because legitimate states themselves are often managed by emissaries of the ultraliberal economy, finance, and

industry (Harper, Sarkozy, Berlusconi), they offer no particular resistance to these problematic modes of operation.

Law still exists, but the constraints it imposes apply to
majorities that do not have access to havens outside the law.
It enables corporations and owners of fortunes to monopo-
lize offshore a situation outside the law that nothing can
challenge, while the norms, regulations, taxes, and other
constraints of the legitimate state continue to weigh on its
citizens as a whole. Those citizens find themselves disquali-
fied in the face of the outlaws who have privileged political
positions offshore. The law thus observed in legalistic states
enables players in offshore law-free conditions to increase
the value of their exclusive activities, as when prohibition in
the United States allowed bootleggers to cash in. This leads
Jean de Maillard to say, laconically: "The law creates value
that crime pockets."[2] The constraints of the legitimate state
condition the relative value added to the free ride of offshore
players and turn out to be an indispensable mechanism in
their alegal or criminal industry. The law of constitutional
states thus borders offshore areas and turns out to be the
condition making possible both the criminal activity and the
accumulation of wealth that occur there.

Once domiciled in tax havens, financial and even
criminal players escape from all control. There is no law to
judge them. There ensues a form of relativism with regard to
crime—a notion now more subjective than ever. According
to a former advisor to the UN on money laundering, Marie-
Christine Dupuis-Danon:

> We are witnessing a troubling confusion between the
> notions of illegality and legality. Globalization, be-
> cause of the ease of transfers it makes possible, has

> brought a growing number of individuals and compa-
> nies to stop asking whether an act is reprehensible *in
> itself*, asking instead whether there is a way of doing it
> with complete legality anywhere in the world.[3]

Tax havens have set in motion the possibility of drafting laws
and disposing of political sovereignty as one pleases.[4]

Far from fighting against this phenomenon, the legalistic state has adapted itself to become merely one of its
components. The codes of legality it enforces confer public
legitimacy on the investor. It guarantees, controls, and limits
access to social respectability. For access to the law and to
the figures guaranteed and supported by the law is costly.
The map of law covers the political territory and saturates
it with meaning. It expects to find typical characters whom
citizens seek to resemble or else they will count for little. The
capital at their disposal determines the right of access to the
attractive figures of this gallery of the law: if they are poor,
they remain "simple citizens" with basic prerogatives; if they
are better off, they are "owners," "clients," shareholders," or
"board chairmen," so they can double their interests in the
fictitious figure of the corporate person. In this realm, money
presents itself more than ever as a document that is legal
tender, a key to renting a choice costume in the legal cast
of characters. Law and the state that manages it are guardians of these symbolic inequalities, which count as real inequalities. The prerogatives this system guarantees to those
who have the starring roles in the social cast—potentially
unlimited and securitized capital, credit, symbolic credibility, a political career, higher education—help over time to
accentuate and reproduce the inequalities of access to the
front ranks.

Armed with his various financial levers, the offshore player accedes to the financial and political elite of these "democratic" states as soon as he has the funds to clothe himself in the garments of hierarchical and symbolic worthiness. The state, manager of this realm of the law, administers or refuses aspirants' access to the figurative legal domain.

Rather than emerging as the result of civic and political processes, the legal figures impose themselves from the outset as the starting point from which one might consider acting publicly. Corresponding to a legal figure therefore becomes indispensable for anyone who wants to make his voice heard. The slogan of the financial magazine *Forbes* sums up the criteria that now prevail in law: "Money, Influence, Power."

The legalistic state no longer measures up when it comes to defending the public good. Offshore politics makes its effects felt within traditional jurisdictions. For example, the United States tax system has become a sieve, as John Perkins points out:

> The overall share of federal taxes paid by U.S. corporations is now less than 10 percent, down from 21 percent in 2001, and more than 50 percent during World War II. One-third of America's largest and most profitable corporations paid zero taxes in at least one of the last three years in the new millennium. In 2002 U.S. corporations booked $149 billion in tax-haven countries such as Ireland, Bermuda, Luxembourg, and Singapore.[5]

France, for its part, has created a second category of flags of convenience to retain its few remaining ships, and Quebec has reduced to 9.9 percent—as though it were putting a price tag on something for sale in a store—its paltry tax on private investments.

It goes without saying that the wealthiest—financial institutions, major industries, and other players with an offshore presence—occupy this legal space without encountering much resistance. On the contrary, they find they are guaranteed, on the level of strict legality, the right to the unlimited accumulation of assets and resources and can finance influence peddlers able to persuade the authorities to modify the legitimate state according to their specific interests. When it becomes necessary to clear the public arena of any physical presence contradicting the esthetics of good taste in force in the gallery of the law, then the legitimate state will appear in its "law-and-order" guise. The police or even the army will take its place as the stage designer of this radically legalized state, driving any undesirable element offstage in the name of an arrangement of the public arena and the territory that must correspond in reality to the staging and figurative casting of the legally entitled.

In these circumstances, the elite able to operate offshore has every interest in judicializing the various forms of political involvement so as to set a fee for entry to formal agoras, a fee that only its distinguished members can pay. In practical terms, you can go to court as long as you can count on a lawyer. According to law, lawyers represent not "citizens" but "clients." By definition, a client is an individual or a body with enough capital to secure a service. The professional fees in question can be considerable. Whoever does not have capital cannot count on a legal advisor and therefore, in practice, has no access to justice.

The press, owned by large companies that jealously guard their offshore prerogatives, has also helped to privatize public discourse, or even to vandalize it completely, so as to deprive the public of sensible debates that might possibly concern it. Less serious reporting and a greater number of flashy features now adorn an information "industry" in the process of spectacular decline.

Citizens deprived of any offshore access are forced into solidarity with the oh-so-perfectible regime of the "rule of law." Indeed, the liberal principles that guarantee unlimited rights to private property as well as the gallery of privileged roles are also the principles that underlie the few "fundamental" rights that citizens enjoy: the rights they cherish (with regard to property, labor, personal safety, and civil liberties) are guaranteed by virtue of the principles that also justify the overwhelming superiority of legal figures such as the large landowner, the major owner of capital, the head of a media group, the multinational, the bank, the institutional investor, the financial empire, and other corporate persons. It is hard to amend this law without undermining oneself, hard to recognize it without stagnating historically.

Sovereign players in offshore finance can thus confine themselves to the domain of Law within constitutional jurisdictions and enjoy there the prerogatives reserved for the attractive figures in the gallery of law, then leave that regime when it no longer suits them to take advantage of offshore largesse when it fits better with their secret interests.

13

OFFSHORE SOVEREIGNTY

Finance is the new sovereign. The age has to learn to deal with this new order: states as small on the globe as they are financially powerful are dedicated to secret activities and enable "investors" to shape their own system of sovereignty themselves, according to their wishes. Considered from the point of view of financial clearinghouses, the world power structure appears in its true light. Denis Robert writes, "The list of accounts in a clearinghouse such as Clearstream is a formidable snapshot of the financial planet: an unpublished photo of striking realism. Portugal appears to be one hundredth the size of the Cayman Islands. Luxembourg is one thousand times the size of the African continent."[1]

These ratios appear in speech, with the current tendency to dissolve states into the field of "economies," just as politics disappears in "governance." The fortunes managed by the sovereigns of finance or the financial and industrial groups they lead are in an advantageous competitive position with respect to these "economies." Coca-Cola is an economy in the same way as the George Forrest Group and Brazil are. These economic sovereignties are clearly established in distinct and hierarchically organized levels, these days favoring finance. This has reached the point that one can explicitly envisage transferring prerogatives from the political to the purely economic realm. This is what the French investor Claude Bébéar clearly indicated to an audience of economists and students in Montreal: "Governments and nations must resist the temptations of protectionism at all costs and agree to cede a portion of their sovereignty."[2] The "transfers of sovereignty" mentioned in this speech imply a receiving body that is the milieu of finance itself.

The financial elite, thus released from the bonds of legitimate states, engages in trade on a planetary scale, with the public authorities not taxing its revenues or its suppliers, and not even knowing the magnitude of its wealth or the purpose of its multiple activities. The prerogatives and the financial power developed in offshore political jurisdictions, made to measure for the elite, are historically unprecedented. Claude Bébéar, as head of a think tank that had the nerve to call itself the Institut Montaigne, knows whereof he speaks. The insurance company he used to head, AXA, opened bank accounts in Luxembourg in order to avoid the unpleasantness of taxation. From there it was able to sovereignly dispose of its capital using all the levers that offshore jurisdictions arranged for its purposes. The company was indicted.[3] In September 2009, after seven years of proceedings, the Paris prosecutor asked that the defendant not be tried. The defense, armed with a team of fifty lawyers, was pleased with the news. That the charge of money laundering could not be "established" by the prosecution perhaps had something to do with the complexity of the offshore arrangements involved.

When Claude Bébéar advocates a "transfer of sovereignty" from states to international financial groups, he is trying to reproduce a movement analogous to the movement the theory of sovereignty describes between individuals in the state of nature and state entities on which those individuals confer sovereign authority. This new movement consists of having states as a whole abdicate their power in favor of a higher institution that will represent all of them and will better serve their common interests. The strictly rhetorical aspect of the proposition fades when one recognizes the change of level it is proposing. The innovation at issue deserves close scrutiny. On one hand, it consists of neutralizing the power of public institutions, which was granted to them by an originally sovereign people. On the other, it tends to restore a principle that oddly resembles the state of nature from which, in the modern period, theories of sovereignty have sought to distance themselves.

Historically, theories of sovereignty responded to two central requirements: to conceive a form of government that accounted for the responsibility of individuals and not submission to God, and on that basis to endow political subjects with institutional forms able to protect them from their own passions. In other words, at stake was the freeing of political subjects from submission to a divine order while not allowing for the reciprocal harms characteristic of the state of nature. In the face of their capacity to harm, which the philosophical tradition attributed to human "passions," political subjects were asked to demonstrate reason—that is, on the basis of rational considerations, to collectively abdicate the powers they had in the state of nature and confer them on a common body. This authority guaranteed to the community advantages it would be difficult to secure on one's own, such as security and property rights. But in return, it was necessary to act against oneself, against one's "passions." The expression "theory of sovereignty" is thus understood as a logic of abdication and attribution of power to a higher body because of collective consent to serve the common interest.

Ever since, the question has arisen in different forms: Who leads? Who decides? Dealing with this question has never been simple. If it is up to the "people" to rule, through the intermediary of institutions they have chosen, they are the victim of a philosophical trick, for the story by virtue of which they are tied to the state irrevocably relegates this attribution of power to a fictitious past. Reconstructing the consequences of this discourse in tangible historical sequences, recalling that "the law is born of real battles, victories, massacres, and conquests which can be dated and which have their horrific heroes; the law was born in burning towns and ravaged fields. It was born together with the famous innocents who died at break of day," Michel Foucault recognizes in the theory of sovereignty a discursive method to bring the defeated to swallow the consequences of their defeat, as a matter of consent on their part.[4] "Basically, it does not matter if we have a knife to our throats or if what we want is explicitly formulated or not. For sovereignty to exist, there must be—and this is all there must be—a certain radical will that makes us want to live, even though we cannot do so unless the other is willing to let us live."[5]

History has not been lacking in proposals aiming at providing more scope and energy to popular power as such, but the attempt to embody these principles historically has come up against the sociological difficulty of effectively constituting and recognizing the people. The historian Pierre

Rosanvallon has studied at length the fragility of this construct in the period of the French Revolution:

> Modern society has continued to radicalize the conventional and abstract character of the social bond. The development of conventions and legal fictions is tied to the concern with ensuring equality of treatment among individuals diverse by nature and instituting a shared space for very different men and women. . . . In a democracy, the people no longer have a form. . . . The people do not preexist the act of evoking them and looking for them: they are to be constructed. This contradiction is basically the very heart of politics.

Authority thus draws its power from popular assent, but it turns out to be the *only* guarantor of the terms of that assertion. Authority thus finds itself in a position to itself provide the definition, the imagery, the perimeter, and the identity of the people that grants authority its full legitimacy. Rosanvallon writes, "Democracy is thus doubly inscribed in a system of fiction. Sociologically first, by symbolically reforming an artificial body of the people. But technically as well, because the development of a legitimate state presupposes 'generalizing the social'—abstracting it, if you like—in order to make it governable by universal rules."[6] This debate runs through political modernity: of the existing state bodies, and the multitude making up a people, who leads, who decides, and how?

Offshore sovereignty cuts this historical questioning short. If it indeed is up to the sovereign political authority to give the people its definition, there is only one step separating us from the idea that it can do without the people entirely. This step was taken by the German jurist Carl Schmitt when, through his doctrine of sovereignty, he attempted to move Germany out of the confusion into which it was plunged in the last days of the Weimar Republic.

Schmitt postulates from the outset that, historically, the sovereign is "he who decides on the exception." In other words, the sovereign is defined by his capacity to impose his decisions in the historical course of events. In these circumstances, the constitution of the state at best merely underpins the future decisions of political life by determining who, through his public position, will be authorized to make them and by virtue of what possible counterpowers those decisions may be amended or invalidated.

In this way, we can understand what principles lie behind the development of offshore sovereignty. For, according to Schmitt, the sovereign will be strictly he who has the strength to impose his will on history in a decisive way and without necessarily having to conform to a constitution: "If such action [by the sovereign] is not subject to controls, if it is not hampered in some way by checks and balances, as is the case in a liberal constitution, then it is clear who the sovereign is. He decides whether there is an extreme emergency as well as what must be done to eliminate it."[7]

In *La loi désarmée*, Augustin Simard outlines the historical conditions for this theoretical approach: "A constitution that chose to overlook this question and explicitly denied to any organ the quality of sovereign would not suppress sovereignty as a maleficent power but allow it to advance behind a mask and, at certain critical moments, necessarily allow a body capable of exercising it de facto to spring forth."[8]

Who is the sovereign? Today, on the fringes of legitimate states that clearly give the impression they have lost control over global financial and political forces, one observes that other sovereign powers influence the historical course of events. Who are those who determine history, bend states to their logic, instigate wars in parts of the world where their interests dictate it, and channel financial assets without being accountable to anyone? "We will see immediately who is the sovereign." Indeed, we see immediately that the sovereign is no longer absolutely to be identified with the state. We also see it less publicized because the sovereign is increasingly occupied in exercising hidden power in the unstructured dimensions of offshore areas. Beyond the reach of legal frameworks, the bodies active in tax havens even succeed in exploiting what remains of the rule of law while organizing their power through expedients that have no relation to the rule of law. Banks and investment funds, multinationals, mafias of all kinds, and other corrupt political elites use at will the rule of law—when it can still serve them—or flout it when need be.

"We will see immediately who is the sovereign." It would be hard to be any clearer, but just as hard to see things clearly. The players involved are offshore precisely so we will not know anything of who and what they are, even if we manage here and there to spot a name, sometimes an entity, sometimes the fact of a transaction, through the few affairs that make headlines. Who are they? The secrecy covering operations in tax havens concerns banking operations and data, of course, but also the identity of the holders and beneficiaries that count in history—certainly those of whom Schmitt says that we will recognize their power even though we know little about them. Who is sovereign? That is the political question of the age.

More precisely, this question concerns the regressive character of a sovereignty that has freed itself from the constitutional structures of the state. These formless sovereign players that we see invisibly taking up positions in the blind spots of international law, offshore non-law, or state apparatuses that they end up manipulating directly or indirectly pose a problem, the same problem that preoccupied Spinoza: the state of nature to which they are returning us, the stage when each is a threat to all. Offshore sovereignty proposes to uproot the foundations of the modern concept of sovereignty by evading the constraints that the rational actors of an age were supposed to observe in order to contain their counterindicated psychological inclinations.

> Since all are eager to capture the applause of the populace, each is ready to decry another's reputation. As a result, since the prize at stake is what is esteemed the highest good, there arises a fierce desire to put down one's rivals in whatever way one can, and he who finally emerges victorious prides himself more on having hindered another than on having gained an advantage for himself.[9]

Spinoza presented this logic, which sovereign offshore players tend to make inescapable, as what a people seek to protect themselves against.

The margins of secrecy in force offshore grant whoever worms his way into that realm the opportunity to do harm to the social whole that has conditioned him. Georg Simmel writes, "Secrecy is, among other things, also the sociological expression of moral badness."[10] This opportunity, which comes to the holder of the secret, amounts to what Simmel appropriately calls, years before Carl Schmitt, an "exceptional position" (*Ausnahmestellung*).[11] Secrecy, which consists of extracting oneself from the field of social understanding, grants the one who takes advantage of it the opportunity to appear much more powerful than he is, because whoever tries to understand him will have to demonstrate not rationality but imagination. In such circumstances, difference in social class is enough to magnify the one who has mounted a few rungs up the ladder while keeping the reasons for his rise secret. Counting on imagination alone, the holder of the secret is in a position to exercise considerable influence on social life if he is himself "deep and significant," that is, in the end to bring society to change its rules and modes of operation in accordance with his private interests.[12]

Secrecy means, for the powerful, the fact of being exempt from the social arena, and it is this exceptional position, as Simmel understands it, that, following a thoroughly constitutional logic, the microstates that have set themselves up as tax and judicial havens strive to preserve. For Carl Schmitt, the one who resolves things in an exceptional situation is he who historically is in a position to decide. But in a public framework, the possibility of deciding is shared among all those who possess information; in a democracy, "each should be informed about all the relationships and occurrences with which he is concerned, since this is a condition of his doing his part with reference to them."[13] Today, however, tax havens and clearinghouses place a privileged fringe of players in an exceptional position, insofar as they give themselves every prerogative—the only limits they encounter are those of their combined strength. No body is in a position to rigorously supervise their activities nor even to interpret the hieroglyphs of the clearinghouses. Trade, banking, and financial secrecy seek precisely to shelter those who guard secrecy from any democratic impulses.

As democracies, legitimate states, and modern governments found it increasingly desirable to make public the status of the debt, taxes, and military affairs, and also to publish data related to the administration and the justice system, secret societies saw that as a basis for their development, going so far as to create those parallel political states, tax havens.

Tax havens thus conform in many respects to the definition of the secret society proposed by Simmel in 1908: the depersonalization of members (numbered accounts), relations of trust with respect to technical competence and the capacity to keep quiet (the banality of evil that Sylvain Besson recognizes in offshore sociological structures), and the nearly total absence of traces (evidenced by the activities of the clearinghouses).[14] Tax havens thus are characterized by not only keeping secret what happens in them but also keeping secret which particular individuals participate in the decisions made there.

All that lies behind what Claude Bébéar, advocate of the sovereignty of finance, says about transfers of sovereignty—except that the audience for his speech, invited to abdicate a part of their sovereignty in favor of a guardianship guaranteeing advantages such as "peace," is made up not of people but of states. The level of abstraction is extremely high if one expects bodies that enjoy a fragile transfer of power from those they govern to abdicate in turn a portion of their power in favor of a financial elite acting in view of its profit and fostering exclusively the laissez-faire prescribed by economic competition. And the proposition becomes even more problematic if one takes into account the fact that the beneficiaries of this transfer of sovereignty are working not so much to hold the passions in check as to formally reestablish a field of activity for the ultraliberal economy, placing at the center of its values those very stigmatized passions, notably greed.

The sovereignty of high finance is distinguished from that of legitimate states by the fact that it is not accountable to populations nor required to have any relationship at all with them. Nothing is more contrary to high finance than democracy, even in its most diluted forms. This denial of the people does not remain implicit: when state sovereignties resist the sovereign powers of finance, it is necessarily, according to Bébéar, under the unfortunate pressure of "populations [that] are not always very evolved in economic matters." The people is also continually disparaged by colonial metaphors, reminding us that in our world offshore power plays the political role that the colonial powers played in the past in the global South. Bébéar tells Éric Derosiers, "Today, as soon as I enter the global village, I must agree to negotiate with the other members of the village, whereas when I was alone in the forest with my family, I was the unchallenged chief. But now I am in the village. I have to give up a portion of my sovereignty, but I benefit from all the advantages of the village."[15]

Politically, the expression "sovereignty of finance" here is to be taken literally. It does not derive from a vague metaphor, nor is it the exclusive privilege of such international financial entities as the IMF and the WTO. Financial players that seek to take up the resources of "weak" states, using notions of constitutional and national law, have adopted paradoxical forms of organization: factitious states promoting a caricature of law, specific laws, standards, and modes of supervision provide transnational finance with its political foundation and enable it to overcome legitimate states. It is this negative "sovereignty" that high finance exercises when it massively places its assets and manages its activities in the myriad microstates that constitute tax havens, free ports, and foreign-trade zones around the world.

Offshore sovereignty thus endows those who take advantage of it with at least eight levers enabling them to act decisively on the historical course of events without having to go through the institutions of legitimate states:

- A made-to-order state framework for those perverted states, tax havens, and judicial havens
- A network of financial institutions protected by banking secrecy that is flexible enough to conceal the identity of those involved as well as the assets in question (it sometimes also covers certain virtual banks)
- A clearing system that functions as a private computerized record-keeping service and that encrypts, in a language incomprehensible to any investigating magistrate, global financial and stock transactions (these transactions greatly facilitate the laundering of dirty money as well as political corruption)
- The very existence of transnational corporations, most of which have subsidiaries in these tax havens
- Insurance companies adapted to the needs of those corporations, which overstep the regulations in force in legitimate states (corporations can self-insure and pay very attractive premiums)
- Foreign-trade zones and free ports that make it possible to exploit labor without observing any labor law worthy of the name and to produce without paying heed to environmental protection

• Transportation services (particularly ships flying
  flags of convenience) and arms merchants and the
  services of mercenaries, veritable private armies
  needed for operations intended to appropriate by
  force the natural resources of the global South

It is in this respect that a body established in a state of
convenience does not merely evade taxes. Offshore, its prerogatives make it able to finance itself (banks), to invest its
funds immoderately in fanciful products (hedge funds), to establish its own accounting system (clearinghouses), to insure
itself (captive insurance companies), to manage its industries
(foreign-trade zones), to develop oil fields (friendly dictatorships and political corruption), to conduct wars (transfers of
funds to secret services, illegal arms sales, and the mobilization of mercenaries), to charter vessels (free ports), to launder money (offshore banks again), and to infiltrate political
parties in order to place its representatives at the head of
legitimate states. All types of trade, once characterized as
either "legal" or "illegal" to distinguish between them, are
blended together. The offshore complex thus makes it possible to enjoy the benefits of a political framework, to conduct
untrammeled financial operations, to launder the proceeds
of crime, and to corrupt elected officials or warlords in regions in crisis to secure disputed concessions that are all recorded unofficially, to involve the subsidiaries of companies
that are recognized in legitimate states in these processes, to
insure these activities without troubling about the standards
normally governing that sector, to establish factories in areas where working conditions recall those of the nineteenth
century, to count on low-cost shipping that makes possible
this relocation (which is all the more profitable because

environmental protection and labor law are unknown in these regions), and to engage in military operations or even wars without ever having to rely on national armies.

The Elf trial, which concerned the secret dealings of the oil company in Africa in the 1990s, showed how funds for weapons trafficking, for the secret financing of French political parties, and legal and illegal company funds could freely be blended together.

In the banking sector, the Canadian Imperial Bank of Commerce in Geneva is used by many African dignitaries, while it also has branches open to small savers in the major cities of Canada.

Returning to the case of Heritage Oil, it is, to say the least, intriguing that a specialist in mercenary actions, after being involved in controversial activities in Angola, was able to create an oil company that later obtained a concession straddling the border between Congo and Uganda. One question inevitably arises: what and whom are gas station customers financing when they fill their tanks?[16]

Offshore states are the cornerstone of these activities because by claiming the political status of sovereign states in the same way as legitimate states, they limit the scope of their legitimate counterparts.

Although openly fictitious, the theory of sovereignty plays a fundamental role in the rhetoric of power, tying the legitimacy of its institution to a popular will that is practically decreed. This political-legal argument confines the political subject, who must maintain a relationship of loyalty to this sovereign power, which he experiences as a debt. This link is indispensable. It continuously reminds the subject that he could always rise up against his sovereign, for he always has the capacity to do so, but does not because he lacks the will. And if that is the case, public discourse will not touch on the security, legal, management, and institutional arrangements within which modernity has completely enclosed it, because, it is suggested, the subject has freely consented to the fact of political authority and he is responsible for that choice. This choice is embodied in the institutions of domination that bind him to themselves by virtue of a mysterious "social contract" or some unspoken agreement made between the sovereign and the people. The sovereign thus reminds the subject of his state of voluntary servitude. This rhetorical trick allows him not only to force his subjects to be loyal but also, in the final analysis, to make them accept their quasi-complicity when they find, for example, that they have been conquered by a violent foreign emperor. This political argument ultimately corresponds on a collective scale to a psychological repression mechanism. To arm against the possibility of popular uprisings or conceivable forms of resistance, the conqueror who does not want to designate himself as such presents himself rather as the sovereign who has been chosen, regardless of violence, pillage, humiliation, and his fundamental lack of legitimacy. This construction is necessary to order and is the basis of the law to which people later refer to define themselves and position themselves in relation to power.

The transfer of sovereignty that international high finance calls for is addressed no longer to political subjects but to states themselves. And this further gap makes it hard for finance to create a bond of solidarity, even a factitious one, between it and its subjects in the Caribbean, in the supersecure business districts of metropolises, or in the inaccessible principalities of Europe. Having lost this link to its subjects, it then strives to define a rhetoric able to bring crowds and even states into line. What subject could still be loyal to secret bodies that recognize only the forces of money?

Hence, the discourse of advocates of offshore centers about themselves remains embarrassed and is shot through with aberrations. Because taxation is the contagion to be avoided, the island capital owner is trapped between the "backward populations" of the islands, whom he must keep at bay, and civilizations of European inspiration, which are envious of his assets. Hence the image of the "tax traveler": an escapee from taxation hell finding refuge in the isles of liberty.

Such a preposterous semantic construction touches on what Sigmund Freud called "censorship." This arises to remove from the field of consciousness an assertion that is embarrassing for the self insofar as it risks provoking social disavowal. Freud himself makes explicit the analogy between psychological censorship and the censorship more commonly associated with political writings.[17] Censorship is at the heart of dream work just as the island paradise imagery of palm trees is the dream of high finance, the dream that censors instinctual representations and the actual moral damage caused by its activity. Three stylistic devices recur among the techniques of offshore censorship: sarcasm, euphemism, and pomposity.

Sardonic discourse can be recognized in the apparently casual jokes that the authors of "tourist guides" of taxation feel obliged to make in every paragraph. *Bank Accounts: A World Guide to Confidentiality*, by the Swiss tax consultant Édouard Chambost, is full of offhand remarks, hasty demonstrations, peremptory statements, and unanswerable provocations, all evidence of conspicuous bad faith. For example, legitimate states are based on principles "where the man for whom laws are made is replaced by the jurist and not the reverse. This brings us back after a necessary digression to the problem of banking secrecy, since laws only have the value of the men who apply them."[18]

Euphemism shows up when the international community wishes to mask the ravages of offshore legislation. The term "uncooperative countries" is used to refer to the criminally inspired lawlessness of some states, and the sonorous "incentive to minimize the impact of national taxes on our lives" to designate tax evasion, writes Sylvain Besson.[19]

Pomposity comes to the fore when advocates for offshore states wish suddenly to achieve political legitimacy. Then it is said that the international bodies that are seeking to stanch the offshore hemorrhage are "undemocratic," Swiss banking secrecy is identified with Swiss "values," and the ultraliberal laws of offshore states are described as the last guardians of "liberty." The guide by Grégoire Duhamel is particularly fond of this kind of humor about the tax "inquisition" and "kidnapping" carried out by the European Union and "the rule of law" with "Marxist" reflexes.

When it abandons self-censorship, the offshore political program gives rise to all kinds of excesses. A perfect example is provided by the billionaire Bernard Ecclestone. Since a highly secret meeting in June 2000, he has controlled all the advertising revenue from Formula One racing; his fortune is held by a trust on the island of Jersey, and the funds in the trust openly circulate as far as Switzerland. Ecclestone considers Hitler a historically extremely "effective" head of state and openly declares: "I hate democracy as a political system. It stops you getting things done."[20]

All institutions of power arm themselves with narratives to justify their existence, and the institutions of offshore sovereignty are no exception. The sovereigns of finance so dominate populations that they disregard them; they therefore can hardly adopt such costumes of constitutional states as the "social contract" to tell their stories. They are obliged to generate new discourses or, when that is beyond them, recycle colonial myths. The offshore elite finds itself reduced to using dark humor, that desperate rhetoric that greets the inadmissible with laughter.

Yet the sovereign impact of crowds in history is not totally exhausted. A signal, a mere anecdote, is enough to turn the discreet landscape of financial principalities completely upside down. Liechtenstein, Germany's unofficial tax haven, known to have held the secret funds of Chancellor Helmut Kohl's party when it was in power, was accused by the French parliamentary commission on money laundering of facilitating both money laundering and the traffic in human organs.[21] Despite the seriousness of the accusations, the charge had no effect. But a spark was enough to inflame passions against the country. In 2008, German tax authorities obtained from the secret services a list of taxpayers suspected of fraud. Surprisingly, the haul contained not only petty fraudsters: Klaus Zumwinkel, chairman and chief executive of Deutsche Post, was forced to resign. Prominent sports figures, such as Boris Becker, were also cited. The public was up in arms. Attac branches in Germany, Austria, France, and Switzerland organized a public demonstration in Liechtenstein. The scandal spread throughout Europe. Germany stated its readiness to share information with any country that asked for it, if it had a bilateral judicial assistance treaty with Germany. The Netherlands asked fraudsters to give themselves up. The Canada Revenue Agency opened an investigation of one hundred Canadian taxpayers mentioned in the lists obtained by Germany. Searches and audits were carried out in New Zealand and Australia. There were two hundred French taxpayers on the list; the minister of the economy said he wanted them to be sanctioned, but Deputy Arnaud Montebourg went further: "In Liechtenstein, you're a minister in the morning and a banker in the afternoon."[22] At the same time, the French press pointed out that French president Sarkozy, ex officio co-prince of Andorra, was "the ruler of a tax haven."[23]

Even states that protected their own banking secrecy joined the fray. Belgium offered its cooperation. The United Kingdom followed suit, offering £100,000 to the Germans' informer for a list of one hundred individuals suspected of having committed fraud in the amount of £100 million.[24] The European Union defied ridicule and denounced Liechtenstein despite all the tax havens the Union itself harbored.[25]

Although many of these statements were made for appearances, the tectonic plates moved slightly. Pushed by public opinion, government representatives found themselves capable of criticism in areas where omertà had been the rule. As a result, the representatives of Liechtenstein were visibly troubled and the forces of banking and financial secrecy began to make concessions. "The very harsh tone of the Liechtenstein authorities sounds a little like despair. They fear a massive flight of capital invested in the country, which will be transferred to the Bahamas, to Jersey, or to another more secure tax haven," tax expert Lorenz Jurass of Wiesbaden University said to Agence France-Presse.[26] Switzerland was worried about the diplomatic consequences it might suffer because of the scandal.[27] Monaco asked its European offshore competitors to put an end to the prevailing logic of tax dumping.[28] And even Luxembourg felt obliged to justify itself yet again.[29]

If a political earthquake struck the earth in February 2008, this was because of a rebalancing of three regimes of sovereignty. To the political relations between the sovereign entities of traditional states and their offshore stand-ins was added a shapeless but quite tangible popular sovereignty. Another useless pamphlet, an umpteenth strike for nothing, an always futile demonstration, a stillborn newspaper, a desperate boycott, a pulped book, environmental campaigners unjustly dragged into court—all these demonstrations of the powerlessness of the people, provided they were bold and coherent, well thought out and carefully planned, and even if they were without direct results, would have the possibility of turning into discreet victories in the long term, gains finally seen as self-evident, values no longer open to question. Universal health insurance, the forty-hour week, and free education were never the result of polite discussions conducted in the circles of governance, nor the outcome of enlightened exchanges among an elite of experts.

Sovereignty in the twenty-first century is emerging as a relationship among these three: offshore, public, and popular. These authorities adopt, respectively, the aspect of the outlaw, the state, and anarchy. Not one of these three sovereignties is capable of completely winning out over the others. And it is precisely the historic clash between the three sovereignties—offshore, public, and popular—that makes any historical prediction uncertain. The philosopher Georges Bataille identified sovereignty with the moment when knowledge, mastery, method, or utilitarian application confronted the world, confronted what was unknown: unexpected tears, an unforeseeable common future, the impromptu, the in-commensurable, the instantaneous, the earth-shattering. "Not knowing" is a form of sovereignty.

Offshore sovereignty has as its weakness the clearinghouses to which access must be achieved sooner or later in the name of the public good. Alain Vernay has already pointed out that banking secrecy is the least of the enigmas that attract the adventurers of finance offshore, because something beyond that escapes them, something that verges on the delight in the development of parallel political powers that Vernay calls "black." "It is to the alchemy of violence that tax havens owe the bulk of such transmutations," the virtual development of money into an agent for the repression of the forms of violence related to its acquisition.[30]

Political sovereignty, as Carl Schmitt defined it in a land-mark treatise, is based on the fact that no national constitu-tion can guarantee the use that historically will be made of a decision.

Popular sovereignty is forever shapeless. Pierre Rosanval-lon observes, for example, that the principle of popular sov-ereignty historically found itself lacking sociological bases to impose itself clearly.

Thus, we fundamentally do not know where offshore, public, and popular sovereignty are heading. And not know-ing, not being able to achieve self-determination, conse-quently explains why the relationship between these three kinds of power has never been historically fixed. Nothing in-dicates that any one of these three derivative forms of sov-ereignty can grasp history in a resolutely hegemonic way. Nothing. "Nothing" in the sense that if anything remains of an absolute sovereignty understood as an omnipotence beyond the three refracted sovereignties, it would appear paradoxically in this absence of historical determinism. This is an absolute absence that expresses the obstacle that every elite faces in holding permanent power in history. Sovereignty in itself, beyond these considerations, is time, the long time of history itself blocking the pretension of guaranteeing, exclusively and completely, the effectiveness of any form of power. "Nothing" permanently establishes authority over the time shared by offshore thieves, bodies officially crystallizing the public realm, and populations swept away in their imponderable actions. A sovereign "nothing" describes the "sovereignty" defined by Georges Bataille. This sovereignty of history and time over temporal forms and sudden events derives from a broad way of thinking about political matters. Sovereignty is "nothing" determinate, no more than fate or history itself. Offshore, political, and popular sovereignty are destined to interact with and confront one another according to a historically indeterminate and indeterminable chemistry. They are subject to fate—sovereignty in the historical sense. History remains sovereign insofar as it resists prediction. Out of it, relevant in the long term, comes the impetuous irreverence of populations in the face of offshore kitsch and the perverse methods caused by illegal and criminal finance. No opposition is futile, no battle lost in advance. History has to test itself precisely because no form of domination, no institutional foundation, no method of operation, no decree of power can definitively deliver a verdict on what will come to pass.

14

AN OFFSHORE MASS ESTHETIC

The offshore postcolonial esthetic and dark humor have tried, in a palliative mode and with little success, to mask the spirit of conquest that characterizes the successes of the sovereign financial elite. It remains for them to push the political logic of the age toward the absurdity of an amusing mass-media performance tending to derealize everything, including the organizing forms of our era. Tax havens have appeared in Hollywood movies, in popular novels, and in other distractions. The vulgarity the phenomenon takes on does not justify suspending interest in it. Offshore issues do not occupy a central and recurrent place in the mainstream media, but they are paradoxically found at the center of the plots in popular movies, crime novels, and comic strips. Consumers of such media must frequently base their understanding of the plots they are offered on their intuitive or manifest knowledge of tax havens and the multiple facets that define them. In the end, rather than relegating to the rank of mediocrity all works for a popular audience or condemning mass art as such, the issue is to note that this register is, in our "democracies," practically the only one that is able to deal with the subject directly and with almost all its complexities. It is exclusively under the rubric of entertainment that public discussion of the offshore phenomenon is tolerated as a cathartic process.

Fritz Lang clearly anticipated these concerns. In the 1928 film *Spies*—a work in the same spirit as his series of films about Dr. Mabuse—he features a master of mystification playing a double game as president of a bank and a Mafia godfather. He moves easily between the shady world and the honorable sphere of high finance. Postindustrialism is on the way. Being rich and anonymous represents a mode of domination that has little in common with the conspicuous methods of Henry Ford that defined the assembly-line production system. In *Spies*, it is possible to split oneself into several characters, to protect one's interests in various disguises, and to grow rich in complete secrecy. Lang multiplies the social masks his protagonist assumes and discards like so many costumes. This can be seen as the intuition of a man of genius, for it took years before tax havens made their appearance in cinema.

As a matter of fact, tax havens and popular movies share a common history. Alain Vernay points out that even before tax havens appeared explicitly in films, such havens often financed those films: "Tax havens made their appearance in cinema anonymously after World War II when producers shot in countries where they had funds blocked or where funds could be unblocked. For example, Tangiers provided mosques and deserts for British producers without being identified." Countless James Bond films took place in exotic locales before the offshore phenomenon itself was accepted on the big screen, the most spectacular example being *Thunderball* in 1965.

But the plots did more to conceal the way the offshore system functioned than to reveal it. They were content to dwell on the sparkling surface. Travel agencies did their part to make these exotic offshore adventures commonplace. And that has continued into the present. It might be said that the recent *Casino Royale*, adapting the figure of James Bond in the Bahamas to current tastes, closes the circle—at least until exotic license takes the macabre form of sexual tourism in paradises embodying rather than merely representing brutal sensual pleasure.

The presence of tax havens in popular movies has intensified as paper currency—once so photogenic—has given way to digital money and seductive offshore accounts. As time has passed, money in the form of bills wrapped in bundles carried in discreet valises became too cumbersome, as much in the real world of financial crime as in Hollywood plots. The valise full of banknotes, which featured in the history of cinema as a cliché valued by screenwriters because it enabled them to indicate in the blink of an eye the fact of a shady transaction, became in time the emblem of petty robbery and low-level crime. Those who respected themselves were able to open offshore accounts and use computers. Brian Gibson made this explicit in his 1990 TV miniseries *Drug Wars*: when a thief is asked to pay for a shipment of cocaine with bundles of bills, he asks, "What about security?" The cat-and-mouse game between drug traffickers and narcotics agents revolves around offshore accounts in the Caymans, Luxembourg, and Panama.

Ill-gotten gains are no longer symbolized by the dough that can be grasped physically, but by immaterial evocations:

numbered accounts, financial centers that no one goes to, anonymous account holders.

Because Hollywood studios work this way out of a concern for probability, their movies can serve as an indicator of the current state of knowledge of the problem. The public would no longer find it plausible that a powerful figure would bother to lug suitcases full of cash around. Since Fritz Lang, such a figure must also embody wealth through his specific know-how, which enables him to encrypt signs virtually and in a refracted fashion.

It is not surprising that artistic works intended for a mass audience go beyond journalism and freely admit the offshore problem into their plots. Aristotle writes, "Poetry deals with general truths, history with specific events. The latter are, for example, what Alcibiades did or suffered, while general truths are the kind of thing which a certain type of person would probably or inevitably do."[1] Not that the offshore stories of contemporary films fully meet the criteria of probability; many adventure films are full of fanciful plot twists, but they cannot disregard contemporary computer, political, and legal technologies.

Among crime networks, drug trafficking is, of course, a prime example. Franc Reyes's 2002 *Empire* tells the story of a Bronx drug dealer who teams up with an experienced stock market speculator. The dealer learns how to launder and reinvest his dirty money on the basis of his distinguished partner's advice, while the speculator appreciates the new computer-based means of access to the accounts that in the past he had to activate by traveling personally to the offshore branches: "No more planes to the Cayman Islands."

But in the movies, accounting devices in tax havens are

used to plan arms trafficking. In 2006, Andrew Niccol's *Lord of War* described the maneuvers by which an astute arms merchant managed to outsmart international embargos thanks to the places where his ships were registered.

The dispassionate management of sex trafficking is approached in an episode of the comic book series *Largo Winch* by Philippe Francq and Jean van Hamme. This series illustrates the adventures of a young billionaire, heir to the fortune of his adoptive father, who, through a Liechtenstein holding company, runs a conglomerate of companies in media, mining, oil, finance, aircraft, and tourism. Number 11 in the series goes particularly far, presenting the investor confronting the managers of his own movie studios, secretly implicated in prostitution networks run from the Cayman Islands.

Another comic book series, *CH Confidential* by Daniel Ceppi, has a plot involving traffic in toxic or explosive products, piloted from Geneva. The Italian Mafia turns out to be involved, and secret agents have to deal with post office boxes and other forms of shell corporation.

And *Blood Diamond* by Edward Zwick, released in 2006, reveals the duplicity of the diamond magnate Van de Kaap, who, while officially supporting the fight against diamond smuggling that finances wars (the unnamed Kimberley Process), remains the principal participant in the trade through an intricate series of holding companies and offshore bank accounts.

By now, the number of crime novels, films, and comic books telling tales of tax evasion and money laundering is countless. Plot manipulations usually confront the reader with antiheroes and some casuistry. *The Firm* by John Grisham features a Harvard Business School graduate who ends up in a luxurious office controlled by the Mafia; *The International* by Tom Tykwer, released in 2009, exposes money-laundering operations and influence peddling by the International Bank of Business and Credit in countries of the South; *The Deal* by Harvey Kahn, released in 2005, presents the battle of a broker against his associates to block a money-laundering operation involving oil trafficking in a region under embargo. The same thing turns up in a comic book, *Secrets bancaires* by Philippe Richelle and Pierre Wachs: a small businessman finds himself involved against his will in a money-laundering process. The authors give a cartoon version of the sterile administrative procedures under which banks are obliged to ask their clients to certify that the sums they deposit are not dirty money.

In popular movies, Switzerland is the identifying marker for offshore misappropriation. Since the hilarious *Swiss Conspiracy* of 1976, such films as Steven Spielberg's *Munich* and Robert de Niro's *The Good Shepherd*, both released in 2005, have continued to present the Swiss Confederation as the preferred location for the necessary transactions of the secret services of various periods. The same thing is true for the comic book *Diamants* by Agnès Bartoll and Bernard Kölle (2007) and the novel *Numbered Account* by Christopher Reich.[2] One of the adventures of the intrepid United States Treasury agent in the comic book series *IR$* by Bernard Vrancken and Stepen Desberg points up the responsibility of Swiss banks in the confiscation of Jewish assets during World War II.[3] This comic book series does not leave out many financial centers of the sort, starting with Liechtenstein, where the hero's holding company is located. The comic book series *Section financière* by Richard Malka and Andrea Mutti inquires into misappropriated funds from the IMF in Russia. *Runaway Jury*, a 2003 film by Gary Fleder, based on the 1996 novel by John Grisham, deals with influence peddling in the Cayman Islands. In D.J. Caruso's 2005 film *Two for the Money* the protagonist evades United States laws against betting on sporting events by conducting his business in Puerto Rico. By activating his offshore accounts, the protagonist of Oliver Stone's *Wall Street* carries out the most spectacular insider trading activities of 1987. The bizarre plot of *Deception* revolves around embezzled funds that go through Spain to end up in Hong Kong. In Stephen Gaghan's *Syriana*, released in 2006, a tricky merger of oil companies takes place against an urban backdrop: we see the sign "Arab Bank (Switzerland)." The novel *L'ange au berceau* by Serge Lamothe seeks the historical relationships linking today's offshore corporate lawyers to the first scoundrels of modern finance who had cobbled together legal escape hatches.[4] Henri Verneuil's 1982 film *Mille Milliards de Dollars* features a long didactic scene explaining how the head of a multinational goes about cheating the tax collector. By using the method known as "transfer pricing," he ensures that his company's profits are recorded in Switzerland, where they will not be taxed. He also relocates production facilities to Switzerland because workers' rights are not well protected there.

Various films relating the exploits of James Bond, a B-movie such as *After the Sunset* (Brett Ratner, 2004), and the thriller *Undone* by Michael Kimball (1997) present characters on the run from the law in offshore centers. It is a cliché of action movies. An analogy can even be found in a science fiction movie such as *Star Wars*. The first episode, *The Phantom Menace*, presents in the opening credits a dispute about the system of "taxation of trade routes in the galaxy." In the interstices of this interstellar tax system havens are developed for criminals on the run.

Usually, in these fictional accounts, few offshore players seem troubled by the anti-money-laundering measures of legitimate states. Moreover, in *Secrets bancaires* by Richelle and Wachs, they openly mock the "formalities" required by law.[5]

While children are given adventure stories to read exposing them de facto to the hucksters of Liechtenstein and the thieves of Luxembourg, journalists are recurrently taken aback when the bankruptcy of Parmalat, President Sarkozy's vacation, or a huge tax fraud forces Europe to become aware of the offshore phenomenon. It's the world turned upside down. In the 1960s, the Situationists twisted products of mass culture—war movies or action comics—by dubbing the films or using the speech balloons in the comics to present political ideas, in a kind of popular palimpsest, to give them an unexpected subversive cast. Maurice Lemaître, for example, in *Can the Dialectic Break Bricks?* dubbed the protagonists of a bad kung fu movie to make fun of unions, structuralists, and left-leaning media and praise wildcat strikes and individual enterprises of resistance.

Politics at the time permeated mass art. Today mass art permeates a political field of disconcerting semantic inanity. For instance, it is not the best-selling novelist who relies on the economic press when he decides to tell a tale about criminal activity in the Cayman Islands, but the economic press that mentions "this tax haven made famous by the writer John Grisham" to evoke its reality.[6] But "mass" art does not thereby become "popular" art. It does not at all devote itself to a program of class consciousness as it once might have. It makes offshore a commonplace while the news media constantly pretend to be outraged by it. Mass art makes it pass in the background as an obvious inevitability that we have to come to terms with.

For instance, in the 1980s, the author and huckster who goes by the name Paul-Loup Sulitzer invented the genre of "financial western" with his novels *Money*, *Cash*, and *Fortune*. He exalted the failings of finance to present himself as a star of the perversion of accounting. His *Les Riches* is an attempt to naturalize the greedy tendencies of the age, whereas the narrative of *Money*, for example, driven by an unconcealed desire for money—"I feel my lips name it, I hear my voice calling it: 'Money!'"—narrates the international tribulations of an heir despoiled of his father's fortune. Easy money in Africa, tax fraud and money laundering in Switzerland, secret arrangements in Liechtenstein, and the creation of corporations in the Bahamas are evoked with a passion for wealth. Sulitzer's literary production explicitly refers back to what the author says he has seen or done himself in the course of his fruitful career. In 2000, in fact, he was indicted in a serious case of arms trafficking in Angola involving the oil company Elf and important Françafrique networks (the networks connecting dictators in former French colonies with government and business interests in France). In 2006, he was given a suspended sentence of six months for tax fraud. His only useful contribution was to have inspired a line in a song by Alain Souchon.

The authors of the comic book *IR$* have also not shied away from compromising their critique. The artist who drew the adventures of Larry B. Max, the IRS agent who captures criminals in the most remote corners of the offshore network, provided original drawings to the financial weekly *Challenges* in May 2007, not to track down Vincent Bolloré and other financial hucksters but to depict them in their best light. For the cover, he sketched Nicolas Sarkozy, very close to big business, in connection with the "rupture" Sarkozy was then proposing in tax matters. The editors of *Challenges*, supporters of growth and high finance, had to use some clever rhetorical tricks when the time came to offer their readers an illustrated story on the subject of the generosity of global finance and the necessity for the tax authorities to combat criminal powers in extraterritorial jurisdictions. With the elegance one can imagine, they made the Western tax system responsible for and the author of international offshore centers and renamed the Impôt de Solidarité sur la Fortune (ISF, solidarity tax on wealth) the Incitation à Sortir de la France (incentive to leave France).

IR$ was the subject of extraordinary attention by another economic newspaper in the summer of 2002. *Les Échos* published one of the episodes of the comic book in the form of a serial, offering it as vacation amusement for its readers, although adding critical commentary. They all pretended they were learning something, sometimes with stupefaction, about the illegal trafficking and money laundering inherent in large-scale world business, about which the paper generally was silent. The publisher Lombard and *Les Échos* subsequently continued their collaboration.

Publishers do not seem to grasp the nature of the problems dealt with in their offshore fictions. Glénat, the publisher of *Diamants*, which clearly describes the harsh if not cruel conditions under which independent African miners labor, placed a sticker on the book giving the reader the possibility of winning a diamond. The cover is itself an illustration of shameless exploitation, showing in the background a scene of forced labor under armed surveillance and in the foreground the investor and his agent. The reader is completely detached from the subject by being tempted by the coveted object, as though he suddenly had nothing to do with the plot being illustrated. And this occurred at a time when war diamonds were the subject of intense public attention.

A major counterpoint is provided by the novels of John le Carré, which were among the earliest thoughtful representations of the offshore phenomenon. *The Spy Who Came in from the Cold* was published in 1963 and made into a film two years later. The protagonist, an agent of the British secret service, poses as a financial engineer with the mission of setting up financial arrangements through a network of Swiss and Scandinavian banks enabling his service's agents to operate in the East during the Cold War. Le Carré's work as a whole has a knowledgeable and disabused view of the symptomatic traits of offshore sovereignty.

Since then, some fairly well-intentioned Hollywood productions, mentioned earlier, have critically focused on the prejudices to which tax havens give rise. But overall, awareness of the offshore world has been obliterated much more than it has been developed. Plots that would make it possible to grasp the perverse consequences of the maneuvers they describe get diverted into the obligatory mazes of adventure stories and burdened with all the cinema's crime story clichés, garnished with the usual macho misogyny. Not that it's legitimate to ask for "truth" in fiction, but on the contrary these situations should be fictionalized rather than frozen in worn-out stereotypes that prevent critical thinking and have acquired the status of received truth through repetition.

In all these scenarios, the offshore esthetic reveals what opinion makers seem to consider impossible, namely, that the general public could possibly understand, sometimes in depth, the ins and outs of offshore activity, its fine points, its seriousness, and the unspoken psychology connected to it. The public, about which the word in newsrooms is that it fears any critical discussion of the stock market and that it grows anxious when it confronts critical exposés of the strange phenomenon of the offshore question, is suddenly all ears when Hollywood, more rapidly than any didactic presentation, throws in its face the key to plots such as "Caymans," "offshore," "holding companies," "money laundering operations," and "banking secrecy." Only one small step would be needed to reach the conviction that these financial centers are harmful to the public and to what remains of the benefits the public derives from legitimate states. The esthetic establishment will not take this step, but a political movement freeing itself from the traps of expertise could do it, because the situation has been made favorable by the proliferation of propaganda.

It is characteristic of those who triumph to tell their stories, to congratulate themselves on the basis of their mythology (merit, free enterprise, business sense, financial genius), and to try to give it substance. Varlam Chalamov dubs the fabrications that thugs and criminals have developed in history to ennoble their actions "novels": "These prison hyperboles are the mob's propaganda and publicity material, a material of the greatest importance. These tales are the gangsters' university, the endowed chair of their fearsome science. The young listen to the old and grow strong in their faith."[7] These imaginary presentations exalting their exploits interfere with their own understanding of reality, just as the representation of the Mafia in the movies was able to influence the way some Mafia clans decided to settle scores among themselves.[8] Along the same lines, Alain Vernay has observed that a cheesy esthetic constructed by the public relations departments of offshore banks to "facilitate the identification of visitors to tax havens with their favorite heroes," including James Bond, attracted customers.[9]

The island refuge of financial laissez-faire finds its true place in the virtual world of a reading given by an owner of the 1983 edition of the *Guide des paradis fiscaux* by Chambost, presented by Jean-Luc Godard in *Prénom Carmen*. The frontispiece of the book refers to this insular imaginary world. The cliché of the island with a palm tree covers the reader as though providing psychological protection from what the data he is consulting really imply. The reader is on an island and the island is in his mind. He is moved by these images and they determine his behavior. The romance does not have to be real; it needs only to comfort the imagination of those who have business sense. And this is how it operates. The intended reader of the *Guide* epitomizes a financial elite that tells itself stories. The character in this shot is comforted only mentally by the imagery of the exotic island on the cover of the book. This fiction—the actual cover of the *Guide* adorned with a palm tree and the dark humor that underpins the indecent politics of the book—affects this reader only as fiction, never promising the tangible advent of the world it presents.

15

SECRECY

Banking secrecy propels the elected officials that share in it into a social sphere that is closed off and constructed by them. With respect to the identity of holders of accounts, assets and investments, and participants in transactions, secrecy is not the purpose but the attribute by which a group recognizes itself as a secret society. This secrecy, like the tax and judicial havens on which it is based, is thought of negatively by legitimate states and therefore positively by the select circles that are its virtual denizens. Offshore locations, which are in reality frequented only by a few corporate lawyers and whose original sites are in a sense located in the imagination of those who profit from them, should be understood in esthetic terms. "Offshore" is a code that goes beyond mere accounting procedures; it plays with figures. If one failed to acknowledge that acceding to the fantasy world of outlaw brotherhoods, with feigned or real indifference to ordinary social reality, also motivates offshore investing, one would misunderstand the psychological aspect of the problem. This is what Balzac points out in the preface to the trilogy *L'Histoire des Treize* (History of the Thirteen). Speaking more like a historian than a novelist, Balzac presents the secret society of the "Thirteen Devorants" as a group of associates once involved in shady deeds who have returned to civilian life but are still bound by an oath of eternal loyalty. Balzac says not a word about the crimes they committed, either in the preface that identifies the secret society or in the three novels. The novels themselves present the Thirteen, on the few occasions they assemble and travel together, as an enigma merely glimpsed by dumbfounded bystanders. Balzac understands that the relevance of the secret society has more to do with the fascination it exerts on those who do not belong to it than with what really goes on within it. But as a result, it is important to those who do belong that their society be recounted by nonmembers who project onto it countless hypotheses, rather than to ensure the production of a true account. The society is said to expand the personality of whoever belongs: its members are "sufficiently strong to maintain themselves above the law, bold enough to undertake all things, and fortunate enough to succeed, nearly always, in their undertakings." To say that its members are "inaccessible to fear; trembling neither before princes, nor executioners, not even before innocence" confirms the members' belief in their own boldness. To tell this true story thoroughly imbued with fiction, Balzac relies on an informer, one of the Thirteen Devorants. But neither the informer nor the author intends to present "dramas steeped in blood, comedies filled with terror, romantic tales through which rolled heads mysteriously decapitated," as they might have done. The author has chosen to present "gentler events" that do "honor" to the society of the Thirteen. The novel of the secret society thus recounts the redemption of crimes committed through the beauty of the relations binding the participants and through a "higher morality," the myth of which Chalamov denounced so powerfully. But Balzac is not taken in. *The History of the Thirteen* presents itself from the outset as a fictionalized and "captivating" version of crimes that have never been revealed, with the precaution of "respecting certain susceptibilities," hence softened and incomplete, on the basis of information provided by his informer, one of the Thirteen. Why did he confide his tale? "Perhaps," says Balzac, "in confiding to the author the extraordinary matters which he related to him, this mysterious person may have wished to see them in a manner reproduced, and thus enjoy the emotions they were certain to bring to the hearts of the masses."[1] The pleasure of the select member is to see himself imagined by those who have no access to his position. And this is what Balzac gives to his reader, a version that refers primarily to the imagination of those who participate in these secret lives, to the way they wish to be perceived and envied from the perspective of their discreet clubs.

No reality.

In the same way, the powerful men of secret finance convince themselves of the truth of the myth about them, as soon as it is publicized by those who perceive them. Sometimes they aim more at producing this perception than at working on historical reality. It would be a mistake to reduce the question of secrecy exclusively to banking and judicial techniques. Banking secrecy is not a commodity that is simple to market. It touches on a deeper dimension than the anonymity of account holders, the concealment of funds, and the opacity surrounding transactions. Contrary to the complacent image presented by the guides that brag of its virtues, secrecy has little to do with exile, evasion, travel, tourism, and tax flight. This dubious humor is of no interest in understanding the meaning of secrecy, which serves on the contrary to establish the conditions for generalized forgetfulness, on the basis of which its beneficiaries can still play a role in society.

In this sense, secrecy has a good deal to do with respectability, much more than with methods for concealing funds. From this perspective, contemporary financiers are not pirates because they do not live as recluses. They still need to appear in public and to make a good appearance: secrecy is aimed at prohibiting the mention of anything vexatious and hence at facilitating repression. Banking secrecy serves a qualitative purpose and determines the light in which its practitioners may present themselves. Secrecy in Geneva is not the same as secrecy in Panama City. The banking techniques of the Swiss capital are not very different from those of the British Virgin Islands. But it is better, in public, to rely on the former rather than the latter.

Yet something secret still remains in banking secrecy. For it is constituted in such a way that it technically enables those who are charged with not divulging it to themselves be ignorant of what is going on. The world of banking also has its banality of evil. A number of techniques support the effort of mental restriction and show up clearly in the case of "compartmentalization." Compartmentalization forces the possessor of banking information to reveal it to no one even within his own department, so very few people in an institution can in fact know what the banking activities of a client are. When all is said and done, no one knows or should know. As a result, the Swiss branch of a French bank is not authorized, according to this legislation, to communicate its banking information to the foreign head office under whose authority it operates. Banking secrecy has to institute a form of censorship that Sylvain Besson describes in quasi-novelistic terms:

> At that moment, Kaspar Villigier's face assumed an indefinable expression, suddenly evasive and distant, as though he were pretending not to hear what his neighbor had just said. One can see this same expression, a mixture of momentary deafness and feigned indifference, on the faces of some bankers when one pronounces in front of them the words "tax evasion."

"We don't know" is consequently a recurring but often sincere expression used by Swiss political authorities and financiers. Banking secrecy relieves a funds manager from knowing whether his clients practice tax evasion, cigarette smuggling, or organized crime—they are often "business-men about which nothing is known, except that they are incredibly discreet and incredibly wealthy."[2]

These banking techniques illustrate a larger phenomenon: tax havens are zones of forgetfulness and repression in the clinical sense. They are constituent parts of the psychological apparatus, if that is conceived of as a mechanism that is not strictly confined to private subjectivity or internal morality but also involves social life and institutionalized relationships. We repress on a social scale, using the organizations we give to ourselves. The apparatus of the instinctive economy follows the pattern of the apparatus of the financial economy.

This is what occurs in a scenario described by Jean Ziegler in *Switzerland, the Awful Truth*, in which money amassed in Switzerland is "invested with an almost meta-physical majesty": "The handling of money in Switzerland has a quasi-sacramental character. . . . Anyone who commits the sin of talking too much desecrates the sanctuary; such sacrilege is punishable by law."[3] The relationship to money that secrecy institutes becomes naturalized, so the law seems to apply, after the fact, to confirm an existing reality: the ef-fectively magical and sacred character of money.

This imaginary construction is fundamental. According to Alain Vernay,

> Those who resort to privileged financial countries are men and not just managers. . . . They are perhaps look-ing for something different from what they think they are, considering the amount of profit, the degree of risk, and the duration of the protection in their equa-tion, without recognizing that they also mix in other unknowns that falsify it, irreducible unknowns be-cause the financiers themselves are unaware of them. They relate to who the men are, not what they have."[4]

This statement of the obvious brings up "the limits of technical understanding" in relation to the "physical individ-ual" made "of flesh and blood." The secret remains a secret to the one who holds it.

Banking secrecy perfects money's capacity to isolate its possessor from the transactions he carries out. Pure capital unacquainted with its subject, numbers acting on the apo-litical world stage: the intrinsic anonymity of the particular medium of money matches the incognito of those who se-cretly have it. This intersection occurs in the forbidden layers of pleasure, which may involve their share of cruelty. Georg

Simmel views the matter like this: "Thus, people of otherwise great personal integrity have taken part in establishing the most opaque companies, and many people are inclined to behave with much less moral conscience and in a more dubious fashion in matters dealing purely with money than when there is a question of doing something ethically dubious in other relations."[5] We always have fewer scruples in monetary transactions, by definition disembodied, than in open relations involving concrete operations. Money serves as a screen between conscience and action. Hence, committing the worst in the realm of finance makes possible the quiet expression of secret sadism.

For money to support such a denial of life, it also has to be a guardian of secrets from itself. "Bad conscience is a luxury in which these people cannot indulge," according to a Swiss judge.[6] Banking secrecy supports the effort of repression necessary to silence the hidden reasons that explain its power. Imposing secrecy on others means giving oneself the means to deny the facts behind one's hierarchical position. And because it is not possible to silence what everyone around us would repeatedly remind us of if they could, secrecy is necessary to enable the principal figures involved not to know the actual reasons for their social, political, financial, or military power. They thereby begin the process of mythologizing those reasons and consolidating the existence of those myths.

The wrongful cultivation of secrecy in a society can begin to provoke the worst. "If secrecy is not directly linked to evil, evil is directly linked to secrecy," writes Simmel.[7] And no one will be surprised that it is offshore that the funds from tax evasion are mixed with those from international fraud and organized crime.

Nothing is clear anymore in the now unregulated operation of the economy. It has become perverted to the point that it consists solely of membership in the small number of those who *are* secrecy, that is, who exist once there is a sharing of privileged information. Economic pleasure is located at this stage and largely motivates what follows. But do we still understand ourselves in the psychological depths of money? Do we still hear ourselves beneath the coarse laughter of offshore dark humor? To what vacillating regime are public institutions asked to confide their sovereignty? What does it mean when the elite themselves are taken in by the game? When Bernard Madoff, a reputable New York trader and investor, former chairman of NASDAQ, orchestrates over a period of years a fraud involving more than $50 billion, under the blissful gaze of his peers? When the gangrene reaches the powerful through the legislative irresponsibility of Luxembourg? When the victims are primarily institutional investors and very wealthy individuals? How is it possible to believe in an elite that allows a simple trader such as Jérôme Kerviel to extract €5 billion from a prestigious bank?

Banks themselves admit they no longer know the real nature of their assets. After transforming irresponsible debts into securities sold on the markets in AAA-rated bundles, given the pace of speculation and level of abstraction, they don't know what value those products represent and who is ultimately responsible for them. The philosopher Frédéric Lordon is thoroughly perplexed:

> It should be repeated, because the uninitiated will find it hard to believe, but it's the truth: despite all their expert teams and their arsenals of mathematical models, investors, particularly banks, are incapable of de-

termining the value of the securities they are "stuck" with. Of all the paradoxes of this financial crisis, this is perhaps the most delicious: the institutions that consider themselves at the forefront of contemporary capitalism, who think they have achieved the height of sophistication in the art of trading, and the most refined technique for managing risk, are in the end not even able to answer the most elementary and fundamental question of all economic life: "What is the status of my accounts?"[8]

Starve the legitimate state. Caricature the tax authorities. Organize offshore the economic plunder of the North, and even more easily that of the South. Corrupt the dictatorships of the South and finance the election campaigns of the North. Deregulate the few public bodies still standing. This is the program of the age. Who decides? The sovereign. He is now to be found in the absence of framework that characterizes a deconstructed world, still profitable for the few who organize insecurity. The organizers of secrecy have consolidated a world of factitious doubt and have transformed it into a lucrative market to which they offer appropriate financial products, investments leading to plunder, debts that turn out to be hateful, not to mention massive pollution and war. It turns out that responsibility, in the practical and moral sense, is among those things that it is fitting to maintain secret. Because the elite has lost itself in its own self-glorifying stories, it now shows the world its formidable incompetence.

CONCLUSION:
THE ILLUSION OF A TECHNICAL SOLUTION

Although the complexity of the world may discourage us from practicing politics without help from experts, experts do not practice politics. Despite their pretensions, never in history have experts been sovereigns. Expertise does not saturate reality and in that sense is not thoroughly decisive in history. It does not foresee, decide, or palliate the fact that historically, suddenly a king's head rolls, the stock market collapses on the basis of a fetishized index, women refuse to go back to being housewives after working in industry in wartime, airplanes are sent to crash into New York towers, or a former chairman of NASDAQ fleeces members of his own social class. History answers to its own sovereignty, and unforeseeable events often advance history more certainly than the roundtables by which increasingly technical NGOs seek to promote one or two points of consolation.

Nonetheless, now that the issue of tax havens has appeared on the agendas of international conferences and is a prominent subject in the news media, the debate tends to focus on the mechanism that would be most effective in holding the offshore phenomenon in check.

There are most honest proposals: Tax companies on the basis of a detailed consolidated balance sheet to ensure also including offshore accounts opened in jurisdictions that can be classified as offshore. Declare null and void a transaction whose source and destination cannot be determined. Ensure access by international legal bodies to data recorded in international clearinghouses on trades of securities and assets around the world. It remains to be seen what political and financial interests will make sure these proposals will not soon see the light of day.

There are others, more hypocritical—for example, restrictive methods to induce banks themselves to control their clients. After an investigation in the field, Gilles Favarel-Garrigues, Thierry Godefroy, and Pierre Lascoumes observed the limits of this kind of measure.[1] Or the OECD initiative for a peer review mechanism that would have states observe one another's tax arrangements to put an end to the international hemorrhage of tax revenues. Since most "legitimate states" have long been thoroughly compromised in processes that extraterritorialize and outsource jurisdiction over global finance, when they have not themselves included whole law-free sectors within their own jurisdictions, it is easy to anticipate the kind of discreet understanding they will use to neutralize the mechanism. The fact that a country such as Canada is seen in this context as capable of critical judgment of its "peers," when historically, many members of its elite are responsible for the development of business districts in the most notorious tax havens of the Caribbean, is enough to give an idea of the kind of forbearance that will eventually characterize these evaluations. Not to mention the fact that Canada shares its seat on bodies of the World Bank and the International Monetary Fund with some of these tax havens.

Those who expect better results from the UN will be disappointed. The UN Code of Conduct on Cooperation in Combating International Tax Evasion of 2010 adopts the same premises: there is no question of dismantling tax havens themselves; the combat against tax evasion is internal to legitimate states and will pass through legislative changes adopted by individual states as soon as they have reached agreement in the framework of multilateral negotiations. This will be a delight for connoisseurs of the refined pleasures of lobbying and the witticisms of cabinet ministers' waiting rooms.

These measures are presented by the best-intentioned critics as another "first step in the right direction." People are pleased that the political class has taken hold of the question rather than marginalizing it, as it so often had when, sometimes with its participation, jurisdictions that turned the law inside out were developing. One might believe it. But it also has to be acknowledged that there is a risk in reducing the problem to discussions by experts about measures and arrangements—at the slightest initiative by state institutions, people will hasten to declare tax havens "finished," as French president Nicolas Sarkozy peremptorily stated a few days before the G20 meeting in Pittsburgh in September 2009.

Beyond these debates between experts, a question remains: why attack tax havens primarily through technical methods and usually voluntary mechanisms?

The beneficiaries of offshore prerogatives are players now able to outclass or even to designate the political elite—

banks, international investors, aggressive oil or mining multinationals, arms traffickers. Half the world's financial transactions take place in tax havens. That means that half the funds mobilized around the world not only are exempt from taxation and concealed in evasion sites but also are used for operations freed from any form of control and any legal framework, as those terms are understood (in an increasingly theoretical way, it must be acknowledged) in legitimate states. Then how is it possible seriously to think that the appearance of a new form for bankers to fill out, or the organization of forms of peer review by states that globalization has turned into enforcers of business law and that the age of "governance" has made into brokers for jurisdictional advantages at the service of international capital, can have any historical weight in the face of interests of that kind?

Although tax havens and other jurisdictions of convenience may be only post office boxes for companies and individuals registered there, their arrangements nonetheless confer real historical sovereignty on those who, through them, formally become subjects exempt from any rule of law. From their political position in the City of London, the Bahamas, or Singapore, they rely on a set of levers that enables them to conduct historically decisive operations: political corruption, influence peddling in both North and South, mobilization of mercenaries, shipping, development in foreign-trade zones, mixture of funds from very diverse sources, money laundering in the form of "clean" investments in the states of the North. What defines sovereignty, the capacity to make decisions that have effects on the historical course of events, today characterizes the action of players who formally have no obligation to accept any state supervision at all.

Hence, reducing the definition of the offshore problem and the "solution" to it to technical methods does not measure up to the task, even if, depending on the measures, there might be partial and sectoral advances. Considering the environmental challenges we face, can it be claimed that establishing a network of bicycle trails, recycling trash, and developing a new wastewater treatment technique would resolve the problems of climate change and the hole in the ozone layer?

Destined to hold sway for a long time, regardless of all the technical arrangements intended to contain it, the offshore gangrene calls for the public to reach a new awareness that has nothing to do with one technical adjustment or another but deals with principles underlying the political issues having to do with sovereignty. Who leads, who decides, in the service of what private interests, and to whose detriment? This awareness cannot be restricted to a group assigned to the specific question of the offshore phenomenon in "civil society," but needs to be extended to all categories, from teachers to small businessmen, mayors, and school administrators, who have specific reasons to believe that they are suffering from the underfunding of institutions serving the public good, and from the reduction of the legitimate state to a ruling body guaranteeing the security of the middle classes and the massive investment of criminal funds in the economic system.

NOTES

1. DEATH OF A FISCAL PRINCIPLE

1. Ellen Meiksins Wood, *The Origin of Capitalism: A Longer View* (New York: Verso, 2002), 178ff.

2. Georg Simmel, "The Sociology of Secrecy and of Secret Societies," *American Journal of Sociology* 11 (1906): 441, 469.

3. Ibid., 448.

4. Édouard Chambost, *Bank Accounts: A World Guide to Confidentiality*, trans. Peter Walton and Margaret Thompson (New York: Wiley, 1983), 3, 5. See also Édouard Chambost, *Guide Chambost des paradis fiscaux*, 8th ed. (Lausanne: Favre, 2005).

5. Grégoire Duhamel, *Les Paradis fiscaux* (Paris: Grancher, 2006). Examples in profusion; these are taken from 47, 59, 85, 113, and 303.

6. André Harris and Alain Guilloux, *C'est la lutte fiscale: Une nouvelle lutte des classes* (Paris: Fayard, 1988).

7. Alex Doulis, *My Blue Haven* (Toronto: Uphill, 1997), 1, 3.

8. "Principles of Multinational Taxation," in David K. Eiteman et al., *Multinational Business Finance*, 8th ed. (Reading, MA: Addison Wesley, 1999).

9. Duhamel, *Les Paradis fiscaux*.

10. Simmel, "The Sociology of Secrecy and of Secret Societies," 447, 454.

11. Ibid., 31, 29.

2. RECOLLECTION OF SUPREME POWER

1. Fernand Braudel, *Civilization and Capitalism, 15th–18th Century*, vol. 3: *The Perspective of the World*, trans Siân Reynolds (Berkeley: University of California Press, 1992), 128.

2. Ibid., 145.

3. Ibid., 129.

4. Ibid., 200.

3. THE COLONIAL GENEALOGY OF TAX HAVENS

1. Thierry Godefroy and Pierre Lascoumes, *Le Capitalisme clandestin: L'illusoire régulation des places offshore* (Paris: La Découverte, 2004).

2. David Spurr, *The Rhetoric of Empire: Colonial Discourse in Journalism, Travel Writing, and Imperial Administration* (Durham: Duke University Press, 1993), 33.

3. Catherine Hodeir and Michel Pierre, *L'Exposition coloniale* (Brussels: Complexe, 1991), 67.

4. Roger Boulay, *Kannibals et vahinés: Imagerie des mers du Sud* (La Tour-d'Aigues: Éditions de l'Aube, 2000), 14.

5. Édouard Chambost, *Guide Chambost des paradis fiscaux*, 8th ed. (Lausanne: Favre, 2005).

6. Grégoire Duhamel, *Les Paradis fiscaux* (Paris: Grancher, 2006).

7. The novelist J.M. Coetzee cleverly renewed the genre of island stories with *Foe* (New York: Penguin, 1987).

8. Boulay, *Kannibals et vahinés*, 79.

9. Roger Mouralis, *L'Europe, l'Afrique et la folie* (Paris: Présence Africaine, 1993).

10. Michael Levine, "Mainstream Media: The Drug War Shills," in *Into the Buzzsaw*, ed. Kristina Borjesson (Amherst, NY: Prometheus, 2002).

11. Maurice Cusson and Pierre Tremblay, "Marchés criminels internationaux et analyses stratégiques," in *La Criminalité organisée*, ed. Marcel Leclerc (Paris: La Documentation française, 1996).

4. THE CREATION OF MODERN TAX HAVENS

1. Ronen Palan, *The Offshore World: Sovereign Markets, Virtual Places, and Nomad Millionaires* (Ithaca: Cornell University Press, 2003).

2. Michel Foucault, *Security, Territory, Population: Lectures at the Collège de France, 1977–1978*, ed. Michel Sennelart, trans. Graham Burchell (New York: Picador, 2009), 291, 289.

3. Christian Chavagneux and Ronen Palan, *Les Paradis fiscaux* (Paris: La Découverte, 2006).

4. Ibid.

5. Thierry Godefroy and Pierre Lascoumes, *Le Capitalisme clandestin: L'illusoire régulation des places offshore* (Paris: La Découverte, 2004).

6. Jean Merckaert at the conference "Paradis fiscaux et enfers judiciaries: la justice ou le chaos," Paris, Assemblée nationale, organized by the site Paradisfj.info on May 29, 2009.

7. Jean de Maillard, *Un monde sans loi: La finance criminelle en images* (Paris: Stock, 1998).

8. Chavagneux and Palan, *Les Paradis fiscaux*.

9. Ibid.

10. Ibid.

5. CRIMINAL LAIRS

1. Pino Arlacchi, *Mafia Business: The Mafia Ethic and the Spirit*

of Capitalism, trans. Martin Ryle (New York: Oxford University Press, 1988).

2. Varlam Chalamov, *Essais sur le monde du crime*, trans. Sophie Benech and Lily Denis (Paris: Gallimard, 1993).

3. Arlacchi, *Mafia Business*, 92, 164.

4. Ibid., 146.

5. Marie-Christine Dupuis-Danon, *Finance criminelle: Comment le crime organisé blanchit l'argent sale* (Paris: PUF, 1998).

6. Jean de Maillard, *Un monde sans loi: La finance criminelle en images* (Paris: Stock, 1998).

7. François-Xavier Verschave, *L'Envers de la dette: Criminalité politique au Congo-Brazza et en Angola* (Marseille: Agone, 2003).

8. Michael Levine, "Mainstream Media: The Drug War Shills," in *Into the Buzzsaw*, ed. Kristina Borjesson (Amherst, NY: Prometheus, 2002), 165ff.

9. Michel Taille, "Pernod-Ricard accusé de deal avec les cartels de la cocaïne: Le fabricant d'anisette assigné en justice par la Colombie," *Libération*, July 30, 2007.

10. Karl Laske, "Un été 1998," *Libération*, July 20, 1998.

11. Eva Joly, *Notre affaire à tous* (Paris: Les Arènes, 2000).

12. Marie-Noëlle Terisse, "L'affaire Parmalat ébranle le capitalisme italien," *Le Monde*, December 23, 2003.

13. "Carlo Tanzi détenait un compte à Monaco," *Le Monde* according to Agence France-Presse, January 24, 2004.

14. Sylvain Besson, *L'argent secret des paradis fiscaux* (Paris: Seuil, 2002), 7.

15. Stéphane Mallarmé, "Or," *Œuvres complètes*, ed. Henri Mondor and G. Jean-Aubry (Paris: Gallimard, Bibliothèque de la Pléiade, 1945), 398.

16. François Morin, *Le Nouveau Mur de l'argent: Essai sur la finance globalisée* (Paris: Seuil, 2006).

17. Raymond W. Baker, *Capitalism's Achilles Heel: Dirty Money and How to Renew the Free-Market System* (Hoboken: Wiley, 2005), 162ff.

18. Éric Vernier, symposium "Paradis fiscaux et enfers judiciares: La justice ou le chaos," Paris, Assemblée nationale, May 27, 2009.

19. Denis Robert, *La Boîte noire* (Paris: Les Arènes, 2002), 22, 23.

20. Denis Robert and Ernest Backes, *Révélation$* (Paris: Les Arènes, 2001), 33–34.

21. Ibid.

22. Robert, *La Boîte noire,* 167.

23. Denis Robert, *La Domination du monde* (Paris: Julliard, 2006).

24. Maillard, *Un monde sans loi.*

25. Jean de Maillard, *Le Rapport censuré: Critique non autorisée d'un monde déréglé* (Paris: Flammarion, 2004), 78.

26. This calls into question the position of those who tend to minimize the funds involved in international money-laundering operations by drastically narrowing how they are defined, as Alain Labrousse does in *Géopolitiques des drogues* (Paris: PUF, 2004), cited by Maillard, and by R.T. Naylor in *Wages of Crime: Black Markets, Illegal Finance, and the Underworld Economy,* revised edition (Ithaca: Cornell University Press, 2004), 134, 137.

27 Baker, *Capitalism's Achilles Heel,* 173.

28. Thierry Michel, *Katanga Business,* Belgium, 2009.

29. Naylor, *Wages of Crime,* 196ff.

30. Baker, *Capitalism's Achilles Heel,* 162.

6. A PERFECT UNION BETWEEN LEGITIMATE STATES AND TAX HAVENS

1. *Télérama,* April 16, 2009, quoted in "Les jérémiades de Total," *Billets d'Afrique* 182 (July 2009).

2. Raymond W. Baker, *Capitalism's Achilles Heel: Dirty Money and How to Renew the Free-Market System* (Hoboken: Wiley, 2005), 194.

3. Yves Engler, *The Black Book of Canadian Foreign Policy* (Vancouver: Red Publishing, 2009).

4. Quoted in R.T. Naylor, *Hot Money and the Politics of Debt*, 3rd ed. (Montreal: McGill-Queen's University Press, 2004), 301.

5. "Dirty Laundry," *The Fifth Estate*, Canadian Broadcasting Corporation (CBC), May 13, 1986, quoted in Mario Possamai, *Money on the Run* (Toronto: Viking, 1992), 110.

6. An analysis confirmed by R.T. Naylor, *Hot Money*, 298ff.

7. Oxfam International, *Tax Havens: Releasing the Hidden Billions for Poverty Eradication*, Oxfam Briefing Paper, 2002, 2.

8. Olivier Cyran, "La tourmente financière vue d'un paradis fiscal," *Le Monde diplomatique*, December 2008.

9. "Les îles Caïmans au bord de la faillite," *Les Échos*, September 4, 2009.

10. Lucy Komisar, "The Wall Street ICEcapade," *American Interest*, July–August 2010.

11. Ibid.

12. Thierry Godefroy and Pierre Lascoumes, *Le Capitalisme clandestin: L'illusoire régulation des places offshore* (Paris: La Découverte, 2004), 39–40.

13. Marie-Christine Dupuis-Danon, *Finance criminelle: Comment le crime organisé blanchit l'argent sale*, 2nd ed. (Paris: PUF, 2004), 177.

14. Quoted in Baker, *Capitalism's Achilles Heel*, 37.

15. Godefroy and Lascoumes, *Le Capitalisme clandestin*, 66–67.

16. Patrice Meyzonnier, *Trafics et crimes en Amérique centrale et dans les Caraïbes* (Paris: PUF, 2000), 56.

17. Sylvain Besson, *L'argent secret des paradis fiscaux* (Paris: Seuil, 2002), 146–47.

18. Christophe Lutundula, president, *Commission spéciale chargée de l'examen de la validité des conventions à caractère économique et financier conclues pendant les guerres de 1996–1997 et de 1998–2003* (Kinshasa: Assemblée Nationale, 2003).

7. DENS OF INDUSTRIAL RELOCATION

1. Foreign Investment Advisory Service, www.fias.net, cited in "Zones franches et libre-échange," Groupe de travail ATTAC-Marseille "Paradis fiscaux et zones franches," October 26, 2000.

2. Erwin Wagenhofer, *Let's Make Money* (Austria: Ad Vitam Distribution, 2008).

3. Jean-Pierre Singa Boyenge, *Base de données du BIT* [Bureau International du Travail] *sur les zones franches d'exportation* (Geneva: ILO, 2006), quoted in Oxfam France and Comité contre la faim dans le monde–Terre solidaire, *Des sociétés à irresponsabilités illimitées!: Pour une RSEF (responsabilité sociale environnementale et fiscale) des sociétés multinationals*, Paris, March 2009.

4. Stephanie Black, *Life & Debt*, United States, Tuff Gong Pictures, 2001, as well as on the island's chronic indebtedness, William Karel, *Jamaïque/FMI: Mourir à crédit*, France, Arte, 1996.

5. Naomi Klein, *No Logo* (New York: Picador USA, 1999), 204–6.

6. Alain Deneault, *Paul Martin et compagnies: Soixante thèses sur l'*alégalité *des paradis fiscaux* (Montréal: VLB, 2004), 44.

7. Michael Kot, *Shipbreakers*, National Film Board of Canada, 2004.

8. François Lille and Raphaël Baumler, *Transport maritime: Danger public et bien mondial* (Paris: Charles Léopold Mayer, 2005), 200.

9. United Nations Conference on Trade and Development, *Review of Maritime Transport* (New York and Geneva: United Nations, 2009), www.unctad.org/en/docs/rmt2009_en.pdf.

10. Édouard Chambost, *Guide Chambost des paradis fiscaux*, 8th ed. (Lausanne: Favre, 2005), 543.

11. Khadija Sharife, "Golfe du Mexique: Comment BP se joue de la loi," *Le Monde diplomatique*, July 2010, 1, 19.

12. Ibid.

13. Yobie Benjamin, "Oil Spill Surprise: Who's in Charge of

BP's Oil Rig Safety? Not the USA," *San Francisco Chronicle*, June 15, 2010, www.sfgate.com/cgi-bin/blogs/ybenjamin/detail?entry_id=65798.

14. Lille and Baumler, *Transport maritime*.

15. Alain Deneault, *Paul Martin & Companies: Sixty Theses on the Alegal Nature of Tax Havens*, trans. Rhonda Mullins (Vancouver: Talon Books, 2006), 5–10.

16. Lille and Baumler, *Transport maritime*, 148; "Naufrage d'un cargo en Espagne: 11 disparus au large de la Corogne," Sextan. com, February 27, 2001, http://sextan.com/archives/commerce/kristal_naufrage.htm.

17. Lille and Baumler, *Transport maritime*.

18. André Beauchamp, *Guide mondial des paradis fiscaux* (Paris: Grasset, 1981), 43.

19. Grégoire Duhamel, *Les Paradis fiscaux* (Paris: Grancher, 2006), 651.

20. Lille and Baumler, *Transport maritime*, 148; "Naufrage d'un cargo en Espagne."

21. Gilles Labarthe, "Une catastrophe sanitaire 'sans précédent' en Côte d'Ivoire," DATAS, Geneva, September 6, 2006.

22. Jean de Maillard, "La criminalité financière dessine le monde de demain," *XXI* 2 (Spring 2008): 163.

23. Peter Moreira, "Halifax: A Centre for International Finance? It's No Fish Tale," *Globe and Mail*, November 16, 2006.

24. Marco Van Hees, *Didier Reynders: L'homme qui parle à l'oreille des riches* (Brussels: Aden, 2007).

25. Jean de Maillard, *Un monde sans loi: La finance criminelle en images* (Paris: Stock, 1998), 106.

8. PLUNDER REGISTERED OFFSHORE

1. Michael J. Kavanagh, "U.S. Bill Is 'Embargo' on Congo Minerals, Industry Group Says," *Bloomberg BusinessWeek*, July 17, 2010.

2. Alain Deneault et al., *Noir Canada: Pillage, corruption et criminalité en Afrique* (Montreal: Écosociété, 2008).

3. Films de la Passerelle, Films d'Ici, and RTBF, 2009.

4. John Perkins, *Confessions of an Economic Hit Man* (New York: Plume, 2006).

5. David Rothkopf, *Superclass: The Global Power Elite and the World They Are Making* (New York: Farrar, Straus and Giroux, 2008), 42.

6. Mark Curtis and Tundu Lissu, *A Golden Opportunity? How Tanzania Is Failing to Benefit from Gold Mining*, Christian Council of Tanzania (CCT), National Council of Muslims in Tanzania (BAKWATA), and the Tanzania Episcopal Conference (TEC), financed by Norwegian Church Aid and Christian Aid, March 2008.

7. Oxfam International, "Tax Haven Crackdown Could Deliver $120bn a Year to Fight Poverty," press release, London, March 13, 2009.

8. *Illicit Financial Flows from Africa: Hidden Resources for Development*, Global Financial Integrity, March 2010.

9. DELAWARE, USA: THE DOMESTIC HAVEN

1. Raymond W. Baker, *Capitalism's Achilles Heel: Dirty Money and How to Renew the Free-Market System* (Hoboken: Wiley, 2005), 173.

2. Citizens for Tax Justice, "The American Jobs and Closing Tax Loopholes Act of 2010 (a.k.a. the 'Extenders' Bill) Would Boost the Economy and Improve Tax Fairness," press release, May 21, 2010, www.ctj.org/pdf/extenders2010.pdf.

3. "Barack Obama Backs Crackdown on Tax Havens," *Observer* (London), November 9, 2008.

4. Ryan J. Donmoyer, "Obama Plan on Tax Havens Faces Hurdle in Congress," Bloomberg, May 5, 2009, www.bloomberg.com/apps/news?pid=21070001&sid=aFzDnxkw.984.

5. Charlie Cray, "Obama's Tax Haven Reform: Chump Change," CorpWatch.org, June 15, 2009, www.corpwatch.org /article.php?id=15386.

6. Ibid.

7. "Division of Corporations," State of Delaware web page, http://delaware.gov.

8. "Secrecy Jurisdictions: Mapping the Faultlines, USA (Delaware)," Tax Justice Network.

9. "Haven Hypocrisy," *The Economist*, March 26, 2009.

10. www.axefirm.com, accessed November 4, 2010.

11. Ibid.

12. http://corp.delaware.gov/whyDE_chinese.pdf.

13. Grégoire Duhamel, *Les Paradis fiscaux* (Paris: Grancher, 2006), 625–26.

14. Ashlea Ebeling, "You Don't Have to Move Your Money Offshore to Get Asset Protection," *Forbes Magazine*, August 9, 2010.

15. Pierre-Yves Dugua, "L'État du Delaware, le paradis fiscal américain qui irrite le Luxembourg," *Le Figaro*, April 2, 2009.

16. Justin Häne, "Delaware: Tax Haven or Just 'Advantageous,'" Swissinfo.ch, June 17, 2009.

17. Lynnley Browning, "Critics Call Delaware a Tax Haven," *New York Times*, May 30, 2009, reprinted in *Caymanian Compass*, June 3, 2009.

18. Andrew Clark, "Welcome to Tax-Dodge City, USA: Delaware Offers Corporate Anonymity and Light-Touch Regulation That Rivals Offshore Havens," *The Guardian*, April 10, 2009.

19. Wayne Barrett, "Delaware a Tax Haven for Bloomberg? Oh, Never!" *Village Voice*, June 9, 2009. In passing, the investigative journalist indicates that the entities Bloomberg has registered in the Cayman Islands officially sell their products from

that ultrapermissive tax haven, permitting transfer pricing on very favorable tax terms.

20. Yves Steiner, "Le Delaware, Paradis des firmes suisses," *L'Hebdo*, June 4, 2009.

21. Australian Taxation Office, Australian Government, *Tax Office Submission to US Senate Committee on Homeland Security and Governmental Affairs*, July 21, 2009, www.ato.gov.au/corporate /content.asp?doc=/content/00203526.htm.

22. Other sources were happy with this change in status: "Australia Is a 'Tax Haven' for Temporary Visa Holders," www.bowmantax.com/printerversion.php?category=tax_free_ aust&page=tax_free_aust, accessed November 5, 2010.

23. Myret Zaki, *Le secret bancaire est mort, vive l'évasion fiscale* (Lausanne: Favre, 2010).

24. Jean-Claude Paye, *Global War on Liberty*, trans. James Membrez (New York: Telos, 2007), and "Les trusts anglo-saxons, rois de l'évasion fiscale," *L'Humanité*, April 7, 2009.

25. Stéphane Benoît-Godet, "Secret bancaire: Les Anglo-Saxons contre la Suisse," Abroad-consulting.com, May 11, 2010.

26. Virginie Robert, "Le Delaware, un paradis juridique plutôt que fiscal," *Les Échos*, April 10, 2009.

27. Ibid.

28. Häne, "Delaware: Tax Haven or Just 'Advantageous.'"

29. John G. Edwards, "Officials: Nevada Not Tax Haven: State Leaders Rebut Statement by Premier from Luxembourg," *Las Vegas Review-Journal*, April 4, 2009, www.lvrj.com/business /42466992.html.

30. Ibid.

31. Richard L. Grossman and Frank T. Adams, "Taking Care of Business: Citizenship and the Charter of Incorporation," in *Defying Corporations, Defining Democracy*, ed. Dean Ritz (New York: Apex, 2001), 61.

32. Ibid., 66.

33. Joel Bakan, *The Corporation: The Pathological Pursuit of Profit*

and Power (New York: Free Press, 2005), 13ff, on the "revolutionary transformation" initiated by Delaware and New Jersey, 56 for the testimony of Dr. Hare, also reproduced in "The Pathology of Commerce" section of the documentary based on the book *The Corporation*, directed by Mark Achbar and Jennifer Abbot, Canada, Big Picture Media Corporation, 2003.

34. Georg Simmel, "L'argent dans la culture moderne," in *L'argent dans la culture moderne et autres essais sur l'économie et la vie*, ed. Alain Deneault (Paris: Éditions de la Maison des Sciences Humaines, 2006), 37.

35. Quoted in Bakan, *The Corporation*, 25 and 51, and in the "Monstrous Obligations" section of the documentary *The Corporation*.

36. Emmanuel Lévinas, *Otherwise Than Being, or Beyond Essence*, trans. Alphonso Lingis (Dordrecht: Kluwer, 1991), 27–28, 30.

10. THE COMEDY OF THE "FIGHT AGAINST TAX HAVENS"

1. Most of them contributed to *Un Monde sans loi* by Jean de Maillard, who later wrote on his own *Le Rapport censuré: Critique non autorisée d'un monde déréglé* (Paris: Flammarion, 2004) and *Le Marché fait sa loi: De l'usage du crime par la mondialisation* (Paris: Mille et Une Nuits, 2001). See also the *Déclaration de Paris* by Eva Joly, in Joly and Laurent Beccaria, *Notre affaire à tous* (Paris: Les Arènes, 2000).

2. "All the Presidents Men," Global Witness, March 1, 2002, http://www.globalwitness.org/library/all-presidents-men.

3. "Tax Havens: Releasing the Hidden Billions for Poverty Eradication," 2000.

4. Every year this NGO publishes a Global Corruption Report.

5. François-Xavier Verschave, *L'Envers de la dette: Criminalité politique au Congo-Brazza et en Angola* (Marseille: Agone, 2003).

6. Attac (France), *Les Paradis fiscaux* (Paris: Mille et Une Nuits, 2000); Attac (France) and the Magistrates Union, *En finir avec la criminalité économique et financière* (Paris: Mille et Une Nuits, 2002); Sven Giegold, *Steueroasen: trockenliegen!: Die verborgenen Billionen für Entwicklung und soziale Gerechtigkeit heranziehen* (Hamburg: VSA-Verlag, 2003); and Attac (Québec), *Où va note argent?: Une fiscalité pour les riches* (Montreal: Écosociété, 2006).

7. Alain Labrousse and Michel Koutouzis, *Géopolitique et géostratégies des drogues* (Paris: Economica, 1996).

8. Richard Poulin, *La mondialisation des industries du sexe* (Paris: Imago, 2005).

9. François Lille and Raphaël Baumier, *Transport maritime: Danger public et bien mondial* (Paris: Léopold Meyer, 2005).

10. Denis Robert and Ernest Backes, *Révélation$* (Paris: Les Arènes, 2001).

11. Report of the Committee on Fiscal Affairs, June 2000.

12. "IMF Board Reviews Issues Surrounding Work on Offshore Financial Centers," IMF, Washington, DC, July 26, 2000.

13. Thierry Godefroy and Pierre Lascoumes, *Le Capitalisme clandestin: L'illusoire régulation des places offshore* (Paris: La Découverte, 2004), 156ff.

14. R.A. Gordon, *Tax Havens and Their Use by US Taxpayers: An Overview* (Washington, DC: IRS, 1981).

15. For historical details about these lists, see Godefroy and Lascoumes, *Le Capitalisme clandestin*, 142ff.

16. Quoted by Sylvain Besson, *L'Argent secret des paradis fiscaux* (Paris: Seuil, 2002), 183–84.

17. Godefroy and Lascoumes, *Le Capitalisme clandestin*, 172.

18. Ibid., 199.

19. Judges Bernard Bertossa, Edmundo Bruti Liberati, Gherardo Colombo, Benoît Dejemeppe, Baltasar Garzon Real, Carlos Jimenez Vollarejo, and Renaud van Ruymbeke, "L'Appel

de Genève," reproduced in many printed publications and electronic sites, including the Attac (France) site: www.france.attac
.org/spip.php?rubrique312.

20. "La Nouvelle Fiscalité de l'épargne dans l'Union eu-
ropéenne: Retenue à la source au Luxembourg pour les non-
résidents," Banque Internationale du Luxembourg, July 1, 2005.

21. Grégoire Duhamel, *Les Paradis fiscaux* (Paris: Grancher,
2006).

22. Valentin Petkantchin, "Brussels' Misguided Campaign
Against Tax Havens," *Financial Times*, February 22, 2007.

23. Nicolas Cori, "La Commission juge anticoncurrentiel le
régime des holdings enregistrés dans le pays: Le Luxembourg
perd l'une de ses fenêtres d'évasion fiscale," *Libération*, July 20,
2006.

24. Godefroy and Lascoumes, *Le Capitalisme clandestin*, 108.

25. Duhamel, *Les Paradis fiscaux*, 239.

26. Vincent Peillon, *Les Milliards noirs du blanchiment* (Paris:
Hachette, 2004), 55–56.

27. Christian Chavagneux and Ronen Palan, *Les Paradis fiscaux* (Paris: La Découverte, 2006).

28. William M. Clarke, *The City in the World Economy* (1965;
Harmondsworth: Penguin, 1967).

29. Vincent Peillon, *La Cité de Londres, Gibraltar et les dépen-
dances de la couronne: des centres offshore, des sanctuaires de l'argent sale*
(Paris: La Documentation française, 2002).

30. José Gayoso, *Le G20 de Londres: de la grande illusion à la
pitoyable mascarade* (Rouen: Agglo, 2009).

31. David Servenay, "Bertossa: 'La France n'est plus une
démocratie parlementaire,'" Rue89, May 31, 2009, http://
www.rue89.com/2009/05/31/bertossa-la-france-nest-plus-une-
democratie-parlementaire.

32. Bernard Bertossa and Agathe Duparc, *La Justice, les af-
faires, la corruption* (Paris: Fayard, 2009).

33. Quoted by Besson, *L'Argent secret des paradis fiscaux*, 45.

34. Oxfam International, *Tax Havens: Releasing the Hidden Billions for Poverty Eradication*, Oxfam Briefing Paper, 2002, 2.

35. Among other comical examples, Gerba Malam, "La fin du secret bancaire: Les effets bénéfiques pour l'Afrique," *Afrique Expansion Magazine* (Montreal) 30 (2009): 5.

36. Romain Gubert and Emmanuel Saint-Martin, *"Et surtout, n'en parlez à personne . . .": Au cœur du gang Madoff* (Paris: Albin Michel, 2009), 84.

37. Tabassum Zakaria, "Allen Stanford accusé d'une fraude de 7 milliards," *Le Devoir* (Montreal), June 20, 2009.

38. Gilles Favarel-Garrigues, Thierry Godefroy, and Pierre Lascoumes, *Les Sentinelles de l'argent sale* (Paris: La Découverte, 2009), 276.

39. "Justice: Earl Jones officiellement en faillite," Radio-Canada.ca, August 19, 2009, www.radio-canada.ca/regions /Montreal/2009/08/19/003-Earl-Jones-faillite.shtml.

40. "Fraude pyramidale: Soupçons d'une nouvelle escroquerie," Montreal, Radio-Canada, July 31, 2009; "Chaîne de Ponzi: quatre individus écopent d'amendes de 26 millions," *Le Devoir*, October 27, 2009.

41. "Coup de filet anti-corruption près de New York," *Le Devoir*, July 24, 2009.

42. Peillon, *Les Milliards noirs du blanchiment*, 80ff.

43. Besson, *L'Argent secret des paradis fiscaux*, 167.

44. Marie-Christine Dupuis-Danon, *Finance criminelle: Comment le crime organisé blanchit l'argent sale* (Paris: PUF, 1998), 104.

45. Raymond W. Baker, *Capitalism's Achilles Heel: Dirty Money and How to Renew the Free-Market System* (Hoboken: Wiley, 2005), 173–74.

46. Ibid., 189–90.

47. Favarel-Garrigues, Godefroy, and Lascoumes, *Les Sentinelles de l'argent sale*.

48. R. Kent Weaver, "The Politics of Blame Avoidance," *Journal of Public Policy* 6, no. 4 (1986), quoted in Favarel-

Garrigues, Godefroy, and Lascoumes, *Les Sentinelles de l'argent sale*, 181.

49. Dupuis-Danon, *Finance criminelle*, 104.

50. Michel Surya, *De l'argent: La ruine de la politique* (Paris: Payot, 2000).

11. TWO-HEADED EUROPE

1. François Lille and Raphaël Baumler, *Transport maritime, danger public et bien mondial* (Paris: Charles Léopold Mayer, 2005), 173.

2. Ibid.

3. Jean de Maillard, *Le Marché fait sa loi: De l'usage du crime par la mondialisation* (Paris: Mille et Une Nuits, 2001), 48.

4. *Jeune Afrique/L'Intelligent* 2172 (August 26, 2000).

5. "Clearstream kommt bei EU-Verfahren ohne Bußgeld davon," *Financial Times Deutschland*, January 24, 2004; *Informations européennes*, distributed by the Brussels law firm Astrid Dieskens and Philip Van Doorn, Uettwiller Grelon Gout Canat & Associés.

12. THE REDUCTION OF DEMOCRACIES TO LEGALISTIC STATES

1. Observatoire de l'Europe industrielle, *Europe Inc.: Comment les multinationales construisent l'Europe & l'économie mondiale* (Marseille, Agone, 2005). The European Round Table is a lobby group bringing together heads of major European multinationals. It is involved in all the major decisions of the European Union on economic, financial, social, and environmental matters.

2. Jean de Maillard, "La criminalité financière, face noire de la mondialisation," in *Les Désordres de la finance: Crises boursières, corruption, mondialisation*, ed. Dominique Plihon (Paris: Universalis, 2004), 89.

3. Marie-Christine Dupuis-Danon, *Finance criminelle: Comment le crime organisé blanchit l'argent sale* (Paris: PUF, 1998), 6–7.

4. Raymond W. Baker, *Capitalism's Achilles Heel: Dirty Money and How to Renew the Free-Market System* (Hoboken: Wiley, 2005), 192.

5. John Perkins, *The Secret History of the American Empire: Economic Hit Men, Jackals, and the Truth About Global Corruption* (New York: Dutton, 2007), 294.

13. OFFSHORE SOVEREIGNTY

1. Denis Robert, *La Boîte noire* (Paris: Les Arènes, 2002), 22–23.

2. Éric Desrosiers, "Non au patriotisme économique, dit Claude Bébéar, 'Le développement du commerce est porteur de paix,' croit le président du conseil de surveillance du géant de l'assurance AXA," *Le Devoir*, April 6, 2006. The speech without exchanges with the audience and the press can be found in Claude Bébéar, *L'Investissement international et la souveraineté des États* (Montreal: HEC, 2007)

3. Sylvain Besson, *L'Argent secret des paradis fiscaux* (Paris: Seuil, 2002), 168. See also Gilles Favarel-Garrigues, Thierry Godefroy, and Pierre Lascoumes, *Les Sentinelles de l'argent sale* (Paris: La Découverte, 2009), 114.

4. Michel Foucault, *Society Must Be Defended*, ed. Mauro Bertani and Allesandro Fontana, trans. David Macey (New York: Picador, 2003), 50.

5. Ibid., 96.

6. Pierre Rosanvallon, *Le Peuple introuvable: Histoire de la représentation démocratique en France* (Paris: Gallimard, 1998), 12–18.

7. Carl Schmitt, *Political Theology*, trans. George Schwab (Chicago: University of Chicago Press, 2005), 5, 7.

8. Augustin Simard, *La loi désarmée: Carl Schmitt et la*

controverse légalité/légitimité sous Weimar (Paris: Éditions de la Maison des Sciences Humaines, 2009), 98, citing the remarks of Ernst-Wolfgang Böckenförde, "The Concept of the Political," in *Law as Politics: Carl Schmitt's Critique of Liberalism*, ed. David Dyzenhaus (Durham: Duke University Press, 1998), 42.

9. Spinoza, *Ethics* IV, prop. 58, in *The Essential Spinoza*, ed. Michael L. Morgan, trans. Samuel Shirley (Indianapolis: Hackett, 2006), 131.

10. Georg Simmel, "The Sociology of Secrecy and of Secret Societies," *American Journal of Sociology* 11 (1906): 463.

11. Ibid., 464.

12. Ibid., 465.

13. Ibid., 469.

14. Denis Robert and Ernest Backes, *Révélation$* (Paris: Les Arènes, 2001).

15. Desrosiers, "Non au patriotisme économique, dit Claude Bébéar."

16. Dominic Johnson, "Shifting Sands: Oil Exploration in the Rift Valley and the Congo Conflict," Pole Institute Report (Goma: Pole Institute, 2003).

17. Sigmund Freud, *The Interpretation of Dreams*, trans. James Strachey (New York: Avon, 1965), 175–76, 568.

18. Édouard Chambost, *Bank Accounts: A World Guide to Confidentiality*, trans. Peter Walton and Margaret Thompson (New York: Wiley, 1983), 22.

19. Besson, *L'Argent secret des paradis fiscaux*, 218.

20. Jean-François Nadeau, "Bernie Ecclestone: Attention, chauffard à droite!" *Le Devoir*, July 11, 2009.

21. Élise Vincent, "Liechtenstein, la vallée des milliards cachés," *Le Monde*, February 20, 2008; Vincent Peillon, *Les Milliards noirs du blanchiment* (Paris: Hachette, 2004), 92, and the appendix "Le cas de la principauté du Liechtenstein," in Attac (France), *Les Paradis fiscaux* (Paris: Mille et Une Nuits, 2000).

22. "Arnaud Montebourg: 'Au Liechtenstein, on est minis-

tre le matin et banquier l'après-midi,'" *20 Minutes*, February 27, 2000.

23. "Sulfureux paradis," *Le Monde*, February 28, 2008.

24. Marc Roche, "Sous la pression, le Royaume-Uni modère son projet de taxer les riches étrangers," *Le Monde*, February 14, 2008.

25. Christian Chavagneux and Ronen Palan, "L'Europe en pointe contre les paradis fiscaux," *Les Échos*, February 26, 2008.

26. Dispatch dated February 22, 2008.

27. Agathe Duparc, "La Suisse s'inquiète des conséquences que pourrait susciter l'affaire du Liechtenstein sur ses relations avec le UE," *Le Monde*, February 22, 2008.

28. "Paradis fiscaux: Monaco prêt à coopérer avec l'OCDE si les règles sont appliquées par tous," Télévision Suisse, February 28, 2008.

29. "'Avec la retenue, il n'y a plus d'évasion fiscal,'" *L'Essentiel* (Luxembourg), February 26, 2008.

30. Alain Vernay, *Les Paradis fiscaux* (Paris: Seuil, 1968), 321.

14. AN OFFSHORE MASS ESTHETIC

1. Aristotle, *Poetics*, 1451b5–11.

2. Christopher Reich, *Numbered Account* (New York: Delacorte, 1998).

3. Vrancken and Desberg, *IR$*, vol. 1: *La Voie fiscale* (Brussels: Lombard, 2004).

4. Serge Lamothe, *L'ange au berceau* (Montreal: L'Instant Même, 2002).

5. Philippe Richelle and Pierre Wachs, *Secrets bancaires*, vol. 1.1: *Les associés* (Grenoble: Glénat, 2006), 39.

6. "Les îles Caïmans au bord de la faillite," *Les Échos*, September 4, 2009.

7. Varlam Chalamov, *Essais sur le monde du crime*, trans. Sophie Benech and Lily Denis (Paris: Gallimard, 1993), 157.

8. R.T. Naylor, *Wages of Crime: Black Markets, Illegal Finance, and the Underworld Economy*, rev. ed. (Ithaca: Cornell University Press, 2004), 25.

9. Alain Vernay, *Les Paradis fiscaux* (Paris: Seuil, 1968), 319.

15. SECRECY

1. Honoré de Balzac, *History of the Thirteen*, trans. Katharine Prescott Wormeley and Ellen Marriage (Rockville, MD: Serenity Publishers, 2009), 7–8.

2. Sylvain Besson, *L'Argent secret des paradis fiscaux* (Paris: Seuil, 2002).

3. Jean Ziegler, *Switzerland, the Awful Truth*, trans. Rosemary Sheed Middleton (New York: Harper & Row, 1979), 48.

4. Alain Vernay, *Les Paradis fiscaux* (Paris: Seuil, 1968), 314.

5. Georg Simmel, "L'argent dans la culture moderne," in *L'argent dans la culture moderne et autres essais sur l'économie et la vie*, ed. Alain Deneault (Paris: Éditions de la Maison des Sciences Humaines, 2006), 37.

6. Quoted in Besson, *L'Argent secret des paradis fiscaux*, 161.

7. Simmel, "L'argent dans la culture moderne," 41.

8. Frédéric Lordon, *Jusqu'à quand? Pour en finir avec les crises financières* (Paris: Raisons d'Agir, 2008), 115–16.

CONCLUSION: THE ILLUSION OF A TECHNICAL SOLUTION

1. Gilles Favarel-Garrigues, Thierry Godefroy, and Pierre Lascoumes, *Les Sentinelles de l'argent sale* (Paris: La Découverte, 2009).